101 Ways to Pay Less Tax

Pat Joseph
Iain Watson
Hugh Williams FCA

101 Ways to Pay Less Tax
by Pat Joseph, Iain Watson and Hugh Williams

Lawpack Publishing Limited
76–89 Alscot Road
London SE1 3AW

www.lawpack.co.uk

Printed in Great Britain

ISBN 1 904053 71 8

Exclusion of Liability and Disclaimer

While every effort has been made to ensure that this Lawpack publication provides accurate and expert guidance, it is impossible to predict all the circumstances in which it may be used. Accordingly, neither the publisher, author, retailer, nor any other suppliers shall be liable to any person or entity with respect to any loss or damage caused or alleged to be caused by the information contained in or omitted from this Lawpack publication.

For convenience (and for no other reason) 'him', 'he' and 'his' have been used throughout and should be read to include 'her', 'she' and 'her'.

Contents

About the authors

Hugh Williams FCA is senior partner of H.M. Williams Chartered Accountants and he founded the firm in 1973. He has written a number of books on tax, law and business.

He is also a director of this financial services company, Mitchell Owen Financial Services Ltd, which was founded in 2002 and which works alongside H.M. Williams Chartered Accountants in Plymouth.

Pat Joseph is Assistant Tax Manager at H.M. Williams Chartered Accountants and has extensive experience in tax matters.

Iain Watson is Tax Manager at H.M. Williams Chartered Accountants; formerly with the Inland Revenue, he offers a valuable insider's view of tax legislation.

H.M. Williams Chartered Accountants are recent winners of the prestigious Butterworth Tolley Award for best small to medium UK Tax Team. It has won the coveted *Daily Telegraph*/Energis national customer service award in the small professional and business services category. In 2004, it reached the last three in the national Accountancy Age Awards for the UK's best small accountancy practice.

CHAPTER 1

General principles

1. Put commercial considerations first
2. Working Tax Credits
3. Child Tax Credits
4. Use an accountant
5. Pay tax on time
6. The fundamentals of tax planning
7. Attributes needed by a tax planner
8. How to be a tax planner

1 Put commercial considerations first

Although this may appear to be the wrong foot on which to start a book about saving tax, you should never put sound commercial judgement after saving tax. In other words, it is nearly always the case that it is better to make money and pay tax than to pay no tax but make no money.

Never let the tax tail wag the common sense dog.

2 Working Tax Credits

Working Tax Credits are payable whether or not you have children. So if you have no children or only adult children, don't assume that tax credits are not for you; they could be if your income is low enough. If you are an employee, tax credits are paid with your salary. If you are self-employed, you will receive payments directly from the Inland Revenue.

There are several different parts of the credit, which are paid depending on marital status, the hours worked, your age and whether or not you are disabled. Because of this, there is no 'one size fits all' illustration. However, in most cases where income is below around £15,500 for couples and £11,000 for single people, some credit will be payable if you work 30 hours or more per week. If you are in doubt, it is always best to submit a protective claim (i.e. you can withdraw it later if you subsequently want to) as tax credits are only backdated for three months. This can be done online at www.inlandrevenue.gov.uk or you can contact the tax credit helpline (tel. 0845 300 3900) and ask for a claim form.

3 Child Tax Credits

As with Working Tax Credits, there are various elements to be taken into account. Generally speaking, you can receive credits if your income is up to £50,000 (£66,000 if the child is under one year). It is worth making a protective claim even if your income slightly exceeds these figures.

4 Use an accountant

A qualified accountant will know a lot about what your legal obligations are in terms of taxation and will also know lots of ways to legitimately keep your liabilities to a minimum. Generally speaking, your accountant will save you tax better than if you were dealing with matters yourself, and your accountant's fees may be less than the savings you are making. Provided you do as your accountant asks, you also have the peace of mind of knowing that you have complied with your legal obligations.

5 Pay tax on time

Always pay any tax you owe on time. Interest is charged on late payment at an annualised rate of 6.5 per cent. At current rates, even if you have your money in a high-interest account, it is better to pay the Inland Revenue on time. However, if you are going to go overdrawn by paying the Inland Revenue, particularly if you do not have an authorised facility, then it is cheaper to pay interest to the Revenue than it is to pay interest to your bank.

If your balancing payment (not payments on account) for any given year is paid more than 28 days late, there will be a surcharge of five per cent of the tax still owed at 28 February and a further five per cent will be charged on any sums still not paid by 31 July.

Therefore, if you have to make a balancing payment and a payment on account on 31 January, and you do not have sufficient funds to pay in full, endeavour to settle the balancing payment element by the end of February.

As a general rule, if you owe the Inland Revenue money and are unable to pay, you will generally get more favourable treatment by discussing the matter with Inland Revenue staff rather than burying your head in the sand and avoiding the issue.

6 The fundamentals of tax planning

All taxpayers have the right to arrange their affairs under the law to minimise their liability to tax. This can be done either by choosing a commercial option which generates a lower tax bill than another, or by organising your financial affairs in such a way so as to minimise the tax bill. While there is nothing wrong with using arrangements set up for no other purpose than to avoid tax, it should be borne in mind that such arrangements may not necessarily be in your wider interest, as we have already said.

7 Attributes needed by a tax planner

There are a number of skills required if you are going to plan your tax affairs. These include the following:

1. **The ability to identify a problem:** it may be relatively easy to understand the tax consequences of a problem and even to find a solution. However, the really difficult part is finding out what problems exist in the first place when no-one is there to tell you what they are or even that they exist.
2. **The ability to solve a problem:** even when a problem is identified, not all problems have obvious solutions. Indeed, not all are capable of solution.
3. **Technical knowledge:** don't expect to be a great tax planner if you don't have a sufficiently broad technical knowledge of the subject.
4. **The will to keep your knowledge up to date:** tax is constantly changing. Not only are there annual budgets, finance acts and additional legislation to contend with, but also there are statutory instruments, case decisions, Inland Revenue concessions and ministerial statements, all of which may affect tax planning.
5. **The ability to interpret legislation:** to the lay person, the finance Acts appear to be written in a foreign language, so there is a need to master this alien tongue. The answers to most complex tax problems are not to be found in a text book but in the detailed wording of the relevant sections of the legislation.
6. **The ability and tenacity to win an argument:** this is particularly relevant under self-assessment, where Inland Revenue officials may

have a tendancy to want to place a different interpretation on a set of facts. You will find that it is necessary to sustain or demolish arguments and bring in new lines of attack to convince the tax authorities of your position.

8 How to be a tax planner

1. The best tax planning accountants think of tax planning every time they open a file. If you are not an accountant, the best way to tax plan is to think about it all the time.
2. Tax planning embraces small as well as large issues. Small changes saving a few hundred pounds of tax a year could well produce as large a saving over a period of time as a major tax-planning exercise. Indeed, while you may be able to save your company £10,000 don't forget to look for a personal saving of £1,000 on your own account at the same time.
3. If your affairs are complex, there may be a greater number of opportunities but the complexity may make them obscure. There may be a tendancy for you to forget to look for them but this does not mean that they don't exist.
4. Always read the newspapers because there are often good ideas for saving tax contained in the financial pages.
5. Don't nit-pick too much. A saving of £50 may result in more damage to your mental constitution than is merited by a small increase in your personal bank balance.
6. Ask your accountant to try to help you save tax – that's what most people employ accountants for.

CHAPTER 2

For those with low incomes

9. Become a foster carer

10. Claim tax back on any interest you receive

9 Become a foster carer

There is an exemption from tax if you provide foster care to children and young people who are placed with you by local authorities (HSS trusts in Northern Ireland) or independent fostering providers. The first £10,000 plus £200 per week for each child aged under 11 (£250 for over 11s) is tax free. If the amounts you receive exceed these limits, you can choose between paying tax on the excess or on the gross receipts less expenses. This exemption does not apply to private fostering arrangements.

If you are an adult placement carer in a scheme recognised by the National Association of Adult Placement Services (NAAPS), there are simplified arrangements for calculating your taxable profit. To qualify, you have to provide accommodation and full-time care for between one and three adults, or respite care. The first option is to claim 'rent-a-room' relief (see number 76). The second option is the fixed-expenses method, whereby you deduct fixed expenses for the adults in your care. These amount to £400 per week for the first adult and £250 for the second and third adults. Any amount you receive over and above this is taxable. However, if the fixed expenses exceed your income, you can't claim loss relief.

Remember, whether you foster an adult or child, you are self-employed and may have to pay National Insurance contributions. However, as explained in number 44, it may be worthwhile paying them.

10 Claim tax back on any interest you receive

Don't pay tax if you don't have to. If your bank or building society is deducting tax from interest and your income is less than:

- £4,885 if are under the age of 65;
- £7,090 if you are between 65 and 74;
- £7,220 if you are 75 and over;

you should register to receive gross interest. This is quite straightforward. All you have to do is ask your bank/building society for Form R85 and sign it. If the account is in joint names of husband and wife and only one spouse pays tax, the non-tax-paying spouse can receive gross interest on 50 per cent of the interest.

If your income exceeds the above limits by no more than £2,020, you are only liable to pay tax at ten per cent but the bank/building society has to deduct tax at 20 per cent. You can then reclaim the excess by filling in Form R40 (available from your local tax office or on the Inland Revenue website at www.inlandrevenue.gov.uk).

CHAPTER 3

For those with high incomes

11 The Enterprise Investment Scheme (EIS)

Relief from Income Tax and a potential deferral of Capital Gains Tax are both available when a *qualifying individual* subscribes for *eligible shares* in a *qualifying company* carrying on (or intending to carry on) a *qualifying business activity.*

Now, let's look at what this actually means…

A *qualifying individual* is someone who is not connected with the company, which excludes past or present employees and directors, and anyone who controls more than 30 per cent of the capital.

Eligible shares are new ordinary shares which cannot be redeemed for at least three years.

A *qualifying company* is an unquoted trading company, which can include companies quoted on the Alternative Investment Market (AIM) and which carries on its business activity wholly or mainly within the UK. The company must not have plans to become quoted and the assets of the company must not exceed £15 million immediately before the issue of shares or £16 million immediately after the issue of shares.

A *qualifying business activity* is broadly anything that does not include, to any substantial extent, the following: accountancy services, legal services, finance, banking, insurance, farming, market gardening, property development, forestry and timber production, leasing, letting, operating or managing hotels, guest houses, nursing and residential care homes.

The Inland Revenue will give advance (provisional) approval that the shares will qualify for relief, but that relief will only be due when an EIS3 Certificate has been received from the company.

Investments can be made from the amount of £500 up to a maximum of £200,000 (2005/06) in any tax year. Both husbands and wives have their own limit. If the investment is made before 6 October in a given tax year, up to one half of the amount subscribed for can be carried back to the previous year up to a maximum of £25,000.

Income Tax relief is given at 20 per cent when calculating the investor's tax liability for the year.

If the shares are sold less than three years after they were acquired, then the Income Tax relief is lost. Furthermore, if the investor 'receives value' during the three years, then relief is also lost. There are a number of ways in which an individual can 'receive value' (e.g. by repaying or writing off a debt, making loans or providing other benefits), but this does not include the payment of dividends that do not exceed a normal return on investment.

In addition to the Income Tax relief, there are two valuable Capital Gains Tax exemptions. Firstly, provided that the shares have been held for at least three years, when the shares are sold at a profit there is no charge to Capital Gains Tax.

Secondly, if you have a Capital Gains Tax liability, an investment into EIS shares can be used to defer that gain. A claim may be made for any or all of a chargeable gain arising from any source (subject to the annual investment limits) to be invested into EIS shares within one year before and three years after the disposal. The effect of this is that the capital gain on the amount invested is deferred. The deferred gain does not become chargeable until the shares are sold or until the investment ceases to be eligible (see conditions above). However, where the hitherto deferred gain becomes chargeable, it can be further deferred by the making of a further EIS investment. Successive investments in EIS shares can also create a valuable eligibility for taper relief (see page 66).

Deferred gains do not become chargeable on the death of the investor.

12 Venture Capital Trusts (VCTs)

These are, in simple terms, quoted companies that hold EIS-style investments. The investor is still investing in new and expanding companies but not directly, and therefore has less risk.

Tax relief is due when the shares are subscribed for. The maximum investment in any tax year has been increased to £200,000 for 2004/05 onwards. The rate of relief has been increased from 20 per cent to 40 per cent for 2004/05 and 2005/06.

Dividends from ordinary shares in VCTs are exempt from Income Tax provided that not more than £200,000 of shares in total are acquired in each tax year. The ten per cent tax credit attached to share dividends is still not repayable, but any higher-rate tax liability on the dividends is avoided.

When the VCT investment is sold, there is no liability to Capital Gains Tax on the investment.

VCT investments can, however, no longer be used to defer an existing capital gains liability.

13 Community Investment Tax Relief

The scheme encourages investment in disadvantaged communities by allowing tax relief to individuals and companies which invest through Community Development Finance Institutions (CDFIs). The CDFIs will then invest in businesses and social and community enterprises in under-invested areas. The relief available is 25 per cent of the investment spread over five years (five per cent per year). The investment must be held for a minimum of five years, otherwise the relief may be reduced or withdrawn. There is no upper limit on the amount that can be invested, but there are limits on the amount that can be raised by the CDFIs and that maximum cannot be exceeded.

14 Maximise pension contributions

You get relief at your highest rate of tax for pension contributions. Therefore, if you are a higher-rate taxpayer, it is even more important that you maximise your contributions. The amount you can pay in any given year is dictated by your age, net relevant earnings and whether or not you have elected a basis year. Your basis year can be any tax year in the last five years. For example, you may have had the following income figures from employment or self-employment:

- 2002/03 – £80,000
- 2003/04 – £40,000
- 2004/05 – £60,000

If 2002/03 is your basis year, you can calculate your maximum contributions in 2004/05 or 2005/06; for instance on £80,000 of net relevant earnings.

With effect from 6 April 2006, the basis year rules will cease to apply and new Inland Revenue contribution limits will be introduced.

It is possible to have your contributions paid in one tax year but treated as paid in the previous year. This can be useful if your level of income fluctuates and you have a higher-rate liability in one year but not in the following one.

When contemplating making pension contributions, as with any other investment, it is always important to take good professional advice.

15 What income is free from tax?

- Adoption allowances
- Annuities from gallantry awards
- Attendance Allowance
- Awards for damages
- Bereavement payments
- Bettings and pools winnings
- Car parking benefits
- Child Benefit and allowances
- Child dependency additions
- Christmas bonuses paid by the state to pensioners
- Compensation for loss of office of up to £30,000 (professional advice must be sought)
- Compensation for mis-sold personal pensions
- Compensation for personal injury
- Council Tax rebate
- Disability Living Allowance
- Disability or wounds pensions
- Education grants and awards
- Family Income Supplement and Family Credit
- Gifts for employees from third parties if they are under £250 a year
- Gratuities from the armed forces
- Guardian's Allowance

- Home improvement, repair and insulation grants
- Housing Benefit and Council Tax Benefit
- Incapacity benefit (short-term – lower rate)
- Income Support
- Individual Savings Accounts (ISAs)
- Industrial injury benefits
- Insurance bond withdrawals of up to five per cent per year (this can be complicated and professional advice should be sought)
- Insurance policy benefits for accidents or disability
- Interest from National Savings Certificates
- Interest on delayed tax repayments
- Invalidity pensions
- Jobfinders' Grant
- Life assurance policy bonuses and profits
- Long-service awards of up to £50 for each year of service (for employees)
- Lottery winnings
- Lump sums from an approved pension scheme
- Luncheon vouchers of up to 15p per day but cash would be taxable – this sum hasn't changed for 40 years!
- Maintenance or alimony
- Maternity allowance
- Miners' coal allowance
- National Savings Bank interest of up to £70 per person on ordinary accounts. These accounts are no longer available but the exemption applies to existing account holders
- National Savings Certificates' increase in value
- One Parent Benefit
- Pension Credit
- Pensions from Austria or Germany to victims of Nazi persecution
- Personal equity plans (PEPs)
- Premium bond prizes
- Provident benefits of up to £4,000 for lump-sum payments
- Purchased life annuities – capital element only
- Rent-a-room relief up to £4,250 a year
- Rent and council tax rebates
- Save As You Earn Schemes (SAYE)
- Severe disablement allowances

- Share option profits made under an SAYE scheme – Capital Gains Tax may be payable
- Shares issued on an approved share incentive scheme that has been authorised (professional advice must be sought)
- Sickness benefits under an insurance policy for up to 12 months where the premiums are paid by the employee
- Social fund payments
- Statutory Redundancy Pay
- Strike and unemployment pay from a trade union
- Subsidised or free bus travel to work
- Training allowances
- Vaccine damage lump sums
- Venture Capital Trust dividends
- War Disablement Pensions
- War Widows' Benefit
- Winter fuel payment for pensioners

16 Pension contributions and the over 50s

If you are 50 or over, you can make a pension contribution and elect for it to start paying out immediately.

At its best, a higher-rate taxpayer would make a contribution of £3,600 gross, which would equate to a net contribution after 40 per cent tax relief of £2,160, take a lump sum of £900 (25 per cent of the fund value) and the investment would give a gross pension of about £200 per year every year (depending on age, gender, etc.).

This represents a return of over 15 per cent. Even basic-rate taxpayers would have a return of over ten per cent per annum.

CHAPTER 4
For married couples

17 Equalise your incomes

Husbands and wives should always try to equalise their incomes as far as possible so that one spouse is not paying tax at a higher rate than the other. Investments generating interest and dividends can be either moved to joint ownership, or given entirely to the other spouse. Assets that create income (e.g. rented-out land and property) should similarly be put into joint ownership or transferred entirely to the other spouse.

If you are self-employed and your spouse doesn't work, could you employ him in your business? If so, do make sure that you have a contract of employment, that you observe the National Minimum Wage regulations and that what you pay actually changes hands in a demonstrable way.

Alternatively, provided you can show that your spouse plays a significant role in the business you can make him a partner and then the profits can be shared between you.

In other words, where possible, ensure that the spouse with little or no income utilises the personal tax-free allowance, currently £4,895. This can be achieved by transferring capital either into joint names, where the spouse would get 50 per cent of the income, or into the spouse's sole name. If the capital is cash on deposit, the interest can be paid gross on completion of Form R85, which is available from banks and building societies.

18 Pay your spouse to work in your business

Where a spouse works in the family business and payment of wages can be justified, it is generally beneficial to pay at least the equivalent of the lower earnings limit (currently £82 per week) and up to the tax threshold (currently £94 per week). Not only will this be a tax-deductible expense for the employing spouse, but also it will maintain the employee's National Insurance record for state pension purposes. Assuming there is no other employment, there will be no tax or National Insurance contributions to pay. Remember, the employer will have to send a P60 (a form which shows gross earnings for the tax year) to the Inland Revenue every year so that the National Insurance record can be maintained. Don't forget that you must comply with the minimum wage rates, which are currently £4.85 per hour. The rate increases on 1 October 2005 to £5.05 and to £5.35 on 1 October 2006. The rate for 18 to 21 year olds will increase from £4.10 to £4.25.

This idea is a useful money saver but you have to do things properly. To make things simpler we are going to imagine that you are a married man running a business, but it could be the other way around or, alternatively, it could involve any business person employing anyone who lives with, or is related to, him and who might reasonably be considered to become an employee.

The way it works is that if you employ your wife for (say) £93 per week, if she has no other earnings or income, she will pay no tax on this pay and you, as her employer, will have reduced your tax bill by almost more than £1,000. But do watch the following points:

- You need to record the work that she will be doing and the work has to equate to a real contribution to the business. In other words, you cannot just pay her this money without her doing anything in the business at all – the inspector will not allow the payments as a business expense. We include a form (on page 22) that you and she might complete and sign as being evidence that she is genuinely working. You simply keep this document to present to the inspector if he asks for it.
- As we have just said, you need to watch out for the minimum wage. You would not be allowed to pay her less than that sum, which varies each year.

19 Tax and civil partners

From 6 December 2005, same-sex couples will be able to register their relationship. From this date, all the tax legislation that applies to married couples will also apply to them. For instance, they will be able to transfer assets to each other without incurring any Capital Gains Tax. However, if they have two main residences, they can only have one principal private

A template form proving that your spouse genuinely works in your company

Agreement between:

____

and

____

We, the undersigned, agree that my wife/husband undertakes responsibility for the following activities in my business:

____

____

____

____

____

____

____

It is agreed that for these services my wife/husband will receive the sum of £________________ per year to be paid monthly.

This arrangement is effective from ____________________

____

Signed: ______________________________ Proprietor

Signed: ______________________________ Wife/Husband

Dated: ______________________________

residence exemption, so they may wish to consider making an election to nominate the main residence. They will also be able to transfer assets to each other free of Inheritance Tax.

Throughout this book any reference to married couples will include same-sex couples but only with effect from 6 December 2005.

CHAPTER 5

For employees

20. Claim a flat-rate expense allowance

21. Professional subscriptions

22. Claim incidental expenses when travelling on business

23. Claim expenses against your employment income

24. Claim for the use of your home as an office

25. Submit your Tax Return on time

26. Join the company pension scheme

27. When losing your job

28. Would you pay less tax if you went self-employed?

29. Moving because of your job?

20 Claim a flat-rate expense allowance

Certain employees are entitled to a flat-rate expense allowance to cover items such as special clothing, tools, etc. The list below provides details of how much you can claim. You can claim the allowance for the current year and the previous six years.

	£
Agriculture – All workers	70
Aluminium	
Continual casting and process operators	
De-dimplers	
Driers	
Drill punchers	
Dross unloaders	
Firefighters	
Furnace operators and their helpers	
Leaders	
Mouldmen	
Pourers	
Remelt department labourers	
Roll flatteners	130
Cable hands	
Case makers	
Labourers	
Mates	
Truck drivers and measurers	
Storekeepers	60
Apprentices	45
All other workers	100
Banks – Uniformed employees	40
Brass and copper – All workers	100
Building	
Joiners and carpenters	105
Cement workers	
Roofing felt	
Asphalt labourers	55
Labourers and navvies	40
All other workers	85
Building materials	
Stonemasons	85
Tile makers and labourers	40
All other workers	55
Clothing	
Lace makers	
Hosiery bleachers	
Dyers	
Scourers and knitters	
Knitwear bleachers and dyers	45
All other workers	55
Constructional engineering	
Blacksmiths and their strikers	
Burners	
Caulkers	
Chippers	
Drillers	
Erectors	
Fitters	
Holders-up	
Markers off	
Platers	
Riggers	
Riveters	
Rivet heaters	
Scaffolders	
Sheeters	
Template workers	
Turners and welders	115
Banksmen labourers	
Shophelpers	
Slewers and straighteners	60
Apprentices and storekeepers	45
All other workers	75
Electrical and electricity supply	
Those workers incurring laundry costs only (generally, CEGB employees)	25

All other workers	90
Engineering	
Pattern makers	120
Labourers' supervisory and unskilled workers	60
Apprentices and storekeepers	45
Motor mechanics in garage repair shops	100
All other workers	100
Fire service	
Uniformed firefighters and fire officers	60
Food – All workers	40
Forestry – All workers	70
Glass – All workers	60
Healthcare	
Ambulance staff on active service	110
Nurses	
Midwives	
Chiropodists	
Dental nurses	
Occupational, speech and other therapists	
Orthoptists	
Phlebotomists	
Physiotherapists	
Radiographers	70
Plaster room orderlies	
Hospital porters	
Ward clerks	
Sterile supply workers	
Hospital domestics	
Hospital catering staff	60
Laboratory staff	
Pharmacists	
Pharmacy assistants	45
Heating	
Pipe fitters and plumbers	100
Coverers	
Laggers	
Domestic glaziers	
Heating engineers and their mates	90
All other workers	70
Iron and steel	
Day labourers	
General labourers	
Stockmen	
Timekeepers	
Warehouse staff	
Weighmen	60
Apprentices	45
All other workers	120
Iron mining	
Fillers	
Miners	
Underground workers	100
All other workers	75
Leather	
Curriers (wet workers)	
Fellmongering workers	
Tanning operatives (wet)	55
All other workers	40
Particular engineering	
Pattern makers	120
All chainmakers	
Cleaners	
Galvanisers	
Tinners	
Wire drawers in the wire drawing industry	
Toolmakers in the lock-making industry	100
Apprentices and storekeepers	45
All other workers	60
Police force	
Uniformed police officers (up to and including chief inspectors)	55
Precious metals – All workers	70
Printing – Letter press section using rotary presses	
Electrical engineers	
Electro-typers	
Ink and roller markers	
Machine minders	
Maintenance engineers	
Stereotypers	105
Benchhands	
Compositors	
Readers	
T & E section	

Wireroom operators	
Warehousemen	30
All other workers	70
Prisons	
Uniformed prison officers	55
Dog handlers – Don't forget to claim for your dog	
Public service	
Dock and inland waterways:	
Dockers	
Dredger drivers	
Hopper steerers	55
All other workers	40
Public transport	
Garage hands including cleaners	55
Conductors and drivers	40
Quarrying	
All other workers	70
Railways	
All workers except craftsmen	70
(For craftsmen, see appropriate industry)	
Seamen	
Carpenters (passenger liners)	135
Carpenters (cargo vessels, tankers, coasters and ferries)	130
Shipyards	
Blacksmiths and their strikers	
Boilermakers	
Burners	
Caulkers	
Drillers	
Furnacemen	
Holders-up	
Fitters	
Platers	
Plumbers	
Riveters	
Sheet ironworkers	
Shipwrights	
Tubers	
Welders	115
Labourers	60
Apprentices and storekeepers	45
All other workers	75
Textile prints – All workers	60
Textiles	
Carders	
Carding engineers	
Overlookers	
Technicians in spinning mills	85
All other workers	60
Vehicles	
Builders	
Railway wagon, etc. repairers	
Railway wagon lifters	105
Railway vehicle painters and letterers	
Railway wagon, etc. builders and repairer's assistants	60
All other workers	40
Wood and furniture	
Carpenters	
Cabinet makers	
Joiners	
Wood carvers	
Wood cutting machinists	115
Packing case makers	90
Coopers not providing own tools	
Labourers	
Polishers	
Upholsterers	45
All other workers	75
Artificial limb makers (other than in wood)	
Organ builders	90

21 Professional subscriptions

If you are an employee and you pay professional subscriptions and:

- you are required to do so as a condition of your employment; or
- the activities of the body are directly relevant to your employment;

then provided the professional body is referred to in List 3 (which can be found on the Inland Revenue website at www.inlandrevenue.gov.uk/list3/index.htm), you can claim tax relief for the subscription.

22 Claim incidental expenses when travelling on business

If you are an employee and you have to travel as part of your job, you can claim for your travel costs. This does not include ordinary commuting from home to your normal place of work. However, if you work on a site, i.e. you do not have a normal fixed place of work, you can claim the cost of home to site travel provided the duration of your work at the specific site does not exceed 24 months.

Incidental personal expenses for items such as newspapers, personal phone calls and laundry incurred while away overnight on business trips are tax free providing the employer pays or reimburses no more than £5 per night for UK trips and £10 for overseas trips. If these limits are exceeded, the whole amount is taxable.

The full cost of meals and accommodation while travelling or staying away on business is also an allowable expense.

Rather than claiming actual travelling costs, if you use your own car for business travel, you can claim for business mileage – see number 36 for more information.

23 Claim expenses against your employment income

If you incur extra costs as an employee, keep a record of the details and dates on which the expenditure was incurred, together with the bills, and you may be able to claim it on your Tax Return – see box 1.33 on the Tax Return.

Here are some items that you might be able to claim for, unless they are covered by one of the Inland Revenue's fixed-rate allowances (see number 20) (i.e. you cannot claim more than once):

- Overalls
- Boots
- Helmets
- Gloves
- Protective clothing
- Necessary equipment
- Tool bag
- Tools
- Trade journals and technical books
- Part of your own telephone bill covering calls to customers
- Gifts to customers paid for by yourself which don't cost more than £50
- Fees or subscriptions to an organisation (professional or otherwise) of which you are a member, although the Inland Revenue must approve the organisation
- Journals and publications, etc.

If you have to borrow money to buy equipment that is necessary for your job, then the interest can be claimed as an expense. This does not extend to car loans nor to a bank overdraft or credit card interest.

Elsewhere in this book we cover the fixed allowances you may be able to claim. As we say elsewhere, please note that a number of categories of workers, including healthcare workers, have fixed-rate expenses that they can claim. You may even be able to claim back for earlier years that you haven't already claimed for.

24 Claim for the use of your home as an office

If you are required to work at home and use a specific room for this purpose, you can claim an allowance based on a proportion of the total upkeep. You claim under box 1.35 on the employment pages of the Tax Return.

Alternatively, you can receive the tax-free sum of £2 per week to cover the additional costs of working at home. This is obviously a small figure but doesn't need to be supported by documentary evidence.

25 Submit your Tax Return on time

If you are an employee and have been issued with a Tax Return, submit the completed form to the Revenue by 30 September. Not only will the Revenue calculate your tax liability for you, but if you do owe any tax, it will include it in a later year's tax code provided your employment is continuing.

If an underpayment is included in your tax code, and the amount of extra tax you are paying is causing you hardship, ask the Revenue to spread the repayment over two or three years.

26 Join the company pension scheme

If your employer offers access to a pension scheme, it is almost certainly a good thing to do.

27 When losing your job

If you lose your job, you may be entitled to a tax-free lump sum of up to £30,000. This will apply if you have been made redundant because your job no longer exists. If you are allowed to keep your company car as part of your redundancy package, the market value of the car will be taken into account in calculating the £30,000. Payments in excess of this amount will be taxable as well as payments made in recognition of past services.

Most other lump-sum/ex gratia payments will be taxable unless made as compensation for the company breaching your contract of employment.

However, if your contract of employment gives you a right to compensation when your employment ends, then the lump sum will be taxable regardless of the amount.

28 Would you pay less tax if you went self-employed?

The answer is almost certainly 'yes' because there are many more expenses that you can claim. However, if you are going to go self-employed, you have to do so properly or the Inland Revenue will catch up with you and either you or your deemed employer will suffer the tax. On top of this there will also be backdated National Insurance to pay, interest on the late payments and, on top of that, the taxman will demand a penalty. So do make sure that you get it right.

To help you find out whether the Inland Revenue is likely to accept that you are truly self-employed, here is a set of questions that should give you an idea:

1. Is there a contract of service, i.e. a contract of employment?

   A 'no' answer indicates self-employment.

2. Is there a contract for services, i.e. a notice supplied by the person carrying out the work (A), indicating the nature of goods or services he will provide to B (this need not be written)?

   A 'yes' answer indicates self-employment.

3. Is the person who does the work in business on his own account?

A 'yes' answer indicates self-employment.

4. If the person is in business on his own account, has evidence been provided that this is indeed the case (e.g. copy accounts, the payment of Class 2 National Insurance contributions)?

A 'yes' answer indicates self-employment.

5. Are the hours worked decided by the person doing the work?

A 'yes' answer indicates self-employment.

6. Are the days worked decided by the person doing the work?

A 'yes' answer indicates self-employment.

7. Does the person doing the work decide when to take his own holidays?

A 'yes' answer indicates self-employment.

8. Does the business proprietor supervise the work?

A 'no' answer indicates self-employment.

9. Is the person part and parcel of the business?

A 'no' answer indicates self-employment.

10. Does the person supply tools and/or materials when he carries out the work?

A 'yes' answer indicates self-employment.

11. Does the person doing the work give the business an invoice for the work done?

A 'yes' answer indicates self-employment.

12. Does the business calculate how much to pay the person doing the work and give a payslip?

A 'no' answer indicates self-employment.

13. Is self-employment the intention of both parties?

A 'yes' answer indicates self-employment.

14. Is the person bound by the customer care credo of the business?

A 'no' answer indicates self-employment.

15. Is the person carrying out the work required to wear a uniform or dress tidily at the diktat of the business?

A 'no' answer indicates self-employment.

16. Is the person carrying out the work provided with a car or transport by the business?

A 'no' answer indicates self-employment.

17. In the event of sickness, does the business continue to pay the person while not at work?

A 'no' answer indicates self-employment.

18. Is the person carrying out the work at liberty to work for other businesses?

A 'yes' answer indicates self-employment.

19. Is the person carrying out the work required to work in order to perform a specific task?

A 'yes' answer indicates self-employment.

20. Does the business, on asking this person to carry out work for it, assume any responsibility or liability characteristic of an employment, such as employment protection, employees' liability, pension entitlements, etc.?

A 'no' answer indicates self-employment.

21. Is the person who does the work paid an agreed price per job?

A 'yes' answer indicates self-employment (i.e. he is not paid for the hours he works but for the work carried out).

22. Is the work carried out regularly?

A 'no' answer indicates self-employment.

23. Does the individual work for other people?

A 'yes' answer indicates self-employment.

24. Does the person carrying out the work advertise?

A 'yes' answer indicates self-employment.

25. Does the person carrying out the work have headed stationery?

A 'yes' answer indicates self-employment.

26. Can the person send a substitute? If so, has this ever happened?

A 'yes' answer indicates self-employment.

27. Does the person have to rectify faulty workmanship in his own time and at his own expense?

A 'yes' answer indicates self-employment.

29 Moving because of your job?

If you are moving home because of your job, qualifying removal expenses and benefits are exempt from Income Tax. The maximum tax-free amount is £8,000 per move provided that expenses and benefits are incurred in the period from the date of the job change up to the end of the tax year following the one in which the move occurred.

This applies whether it is a new job with a new employer, a new job with an existing employer or you are continuing your current job but at a new location. Issues of ease of daily travelling from the old and new homes have to be regarded and the expenses have to be reimbursed by your employer. Most of the costs reasonably related to the move, subject to limits, are allowed and full details are in the Inland Revenue booklet *IR134.*

The favourable tax and National Insurance contributions treatment of these payments should make them attractive to employee and employer alike when considering relocation packages.

CHAPTER 6
For employers

30 Short-term employment contracts

If you are an employer, particularly where your business's workload varies significantly throughout the year, do consider having your employees on short-term contracts. This gives you flexibility if you need to reduce the number of staff and avoids you having to make redundancy payments. You are still at liberty to give fresh contracts to those people whose services you wish to retain.

31 Share schemes

Offer your employee shares under one of the many share schemes available. This can be a tax-efficient way of passing a valuable benefit to an employee.

What are the rules if I provide shares and share options for my employees?

Under the Employee Share Ownership Scheme, employees may allocate part of their salary to shares in their employer company ('partnership shares') without paying tax or National Insurance contributions, nor are employers' National Insurance contributions payable. Employers may also give free shares to employees, including extra free shares for employees who have partnership shares ('matching shares'), and the cost of the shares and of running the scheme are tax-deductible. The maximum you can allocate as an employer is £1,500 per year for partnership shares and £3,000 worth of free shares per year, although employers may set lower limits. Note: all types of share issued to employees must be reported to the Inland Revenue on Form 42 within 30 days; failure to so do will entail a fine of £300 per employee.

If the employee takes shares out of the scheme within five years, he is taxed under Schedule E. If the shares remain in the scheme for five years or more, they are free of tax and National Insurance contributions when they are withdrawn.

There are two types of share option scheme: 'Save As You Earn' (SAYE) – linked share option schemes – and Company Share Option Plans. Under an SAYE scheme, contributions of between £5 and £250 per month are paid by the employer under a SAYE contract with a building society or bank. The option to purchase shares using the SAYE funds can normally be exercised after three, five or seven years when the contract ends. No charge to Income Tax arises on the difference between cost and market value when a share option is exercised, nor at the time it is granted.

The scheme enables an option to be granted now to acquire shares at today's price. The price at which the option may be exercised must not normally be less than 80 per cent of the market value of the shares at the time the option is granted.

Under approved non-savings-related share option schemes, the option must not be granted at a discount and the total market value of shares that may be acquired under the option must not exceed £30,000. If these conditions are complied with, there is no tax charge when options are granted. Nor is there a tax charge when the option is exercised, providing options under the scheme are exercised between three and ten years after they are granted, and not more frequently than once in three years.

The costs of running the scheme are tax-deductible.

What are the different schemes for providing shares for employees?

The different schemes are:

- Share Incentive Plans (SIP): Under this scheme, which is also known as an AESOP (All Employee Share Ownership Plan):
    - employers can give up to £3,000 to each employee;
    - employees can buy up to £1,500 worth of shares and, under such circumstances, employers can reward the purchasers with two free shares for each share purchased.
- Savings Related Share Options Schemes (SRSOS):
    - Participants can save up to £250 per month to acquire shares at the end of a three-, five- or seven-year period.

- Enterprise Management Incentive (EMI):
    - Companies with gross assets not exceeding £30 million can grant tax and National Insurance contribution-advantaged share options worth up to £100,000 to any number of employees, subject to a total value of £3 million.
- Company Share Option Plans (CSOP):
    - Up to £30,000 of options each can be granted to any number of employees with tax and National Insurance contribution advantages.
- Schemes outside the Inland Revenue approved range of schemes:
    - These will suffer tax and National Insurance contributions.

Needless to say, professional advice must be sought.

32 File your PAYE Return online

Small employers (those with fewer than 50 employees) will qualify for a tax-free payment of up to £825 if they file their end of year PAYE Returns online. The incentive will be paid as follows:

- 2004/05 – £250
- 2005/06 – £250
- 2006/07 – £150
- 2007/08 – £100
- 2008/09 – £75

The Returns must be completed correctly, filed electronically on time and must meet quality standards. Employers who operate PAYE manually should consider switching – the incentive should cover the cost of a computer and software.

33 Tax-free benefits you can give to employees

Give your employees tax-free benefits, such as:

- a canteen if it is available to everybody;
- car and bike parking at work;
- childcare costs and vouchers – not taxable up to £50 per week;
- company cars, vans, etc. – not taxable for those earning less than £8,500 a year (the £8,500 includes the value of the benefit);
- computer equipment provided for employees on loan – not taxable on the first £2,500 of the computer's value;
- exam prizes – they are not taxable if they are reasonable and not part of the employment contract;
- mileage allowances;
- mobile telephones;
- nurseries and play schemes run by the employer;
- outplacement counselling;
- pension contributions and death-in-service cover;
- relocation expenses – tax free up to £8,000;
- retraining and counselling on leaving employment;
- share incentive schemes – not taxable if approved by the Inland Revenue;
- travel to work on a work's bus;
- workplace sports facilities;
- suggestion scheme awards;
- medical check-ups for employees and their families;
- bicycles provided for employees as long as they are used for travel between home and work and private use is limited.

The benefit to the employer is that the employees get a good deal, while the employer gets tax relief on the expenditure incurred.

CHAPTER 7

Company cars

34. Vans have some tax-saving attractions

35. Company cars

36. Claim-approved mileage allowance payments for your car

37. Avoid the fuel tax charge

38. Own your own car rather than using your employer's

34 Vans have some tax-saving attractions

If you are an employee and are provided with a company car, you pay tax on a standard benefit (if benefit it be) of £500 per year – or on £350 if the van is more than four years old. If the van is shared, then the taxable benefit is spread between the sharers. These sums are much less than the sums payable on company cars.

However, it is even better than this because if you drive a van, and even if you use it for restricted private purposes, there is no tax to pay. You can use it for going to and from work, but other private uses would create the charge. Examples of such other uses that would create a tax charge, according to the Inland Revenue, would be:

- using the van to visit the supermarket twice a week;
- taking it on holiday;
- using it for social activities.

But uses that would not trigger a tax charge include:

- taking rubbish to the tip once or twice a year;
- regularly taking a detour to the newsagent on the way to work;
- calling at the dentist on the way home.

But all that glitters is not gold. All these rates are to be revised in 2007 with the van benefit increasing to £3,000 and a further £500 if fuel is provided – so beware.

Why the Chancellor taxes them so little, and then drops all the charges, but then plans to increase them to figures that are far more than the 2004/05 rates, defeats us!

35 Company cars

The company car tax charge is calculated by referring to the list price of the car when new, plus any additional items fitted and less any capital

Car benefit charges based on CO_2 emissions

CO_2 emissions in grams per kilometre			Tax is based on the following percentage of the price of the car
2006–2007	*2005–2006*	*2004–2005*	%
140	140	145	15*
145	145	150	16*
150	150	155	17*
155	155	160	18*
160	160	165	19*
165	165	170	20*
170	170	175	21*
175	175	180	22*
180	180	185	23*
185	185	190	24*
190	190	195	25*
195	195	200	26*
200	200	205	27*
205	205	210	28*
210	210	215	29*
215	215	220	30*
220	220	225	31*
225	225	230	32*
230	230	235	33**
235	235	240	34***
240	240	245	35****

*	add 3% if car runs solely on diesel
**	add 2% if car runs solely on diesel
***	add 1% if car runs solely on diesel
****	maximum charge so no supplement

Note: The exact CO_2 figure is rounded down to the nearest five grams per kilometre (gm/km).

contributions made by the employee, and the CO_2 emissions (which are shown on the V5 vehicle registration document) for cars registered on or after 1 March 2001 (see the table above). Emission levels can also be found on the internet at the Vehicle Certification Agency's website (www.vca.gov.uk) and that of the Society of Motor Manufacturers and Traders Limited (www.smmt.co.uk).

Diesel cars are subject to a three per cent surcharge unless they meet Euro 4 standards (up to 6 April 2006). From 6 April 2006, the surcharge will no longer apply to all Euro 4 standard diesels registered after 1 January 2006. The three per cent reduction will, however, continue to apply to all Euro 4 diesels registered before 1 January 2006 for the rest of their life. See the Inland Revenue's website for further details.

If a vehicle is not available for the full year (i.e. you did not buy or sell it during the year), then the charge is reduced pro-rata.

Therefore, selecting a car with lower emissions and/or a lower list price will reduce your tax liability.

The Inland Revenue leaflet *IR172* is a good source of information and this can be downloaded from the Revenue website.

If you are self-employed and are going to use a car for business purposes, you can claim enhanced capital allowances (see page 54) if your new car has emissions not exceeding 120 gm/km. You will be able to claim 100 per cent first-year allowances (subject to an adjustment for any private use).

Don't forget that the level of road tax you have to pay is also reduced for lower-emission cars.

36 Claim-approved mileage allowance payments for your car

If you are an employee and you use your own car for business purposes, you can claim back 40p per mile from your employer for the first 10,000 business miles in a tax year and 25p per mile thereafter. If your employer reimburses less than the mileage figure, you can claim the difference in your Tax Return. If you can persuade your employer to pay you an extra 5p per mile for carrying a business passenger, it would also be tax free, but you can't claim it if your employer doesn't pay you for it. If you use a motorbike, you can claim 24p for business mileage and if you use a bicycle, you can claim 20p.

37 Avoid the fuel tax charge

As an employee, if you are required to repay all your own private fuel, keeping a careful and detailed record of every car journey undertaken whether business or private, then you would not have to pay tax on the fuel provided for business purposes. However, you have to bear in mind that travel from home to the place of work is considered to be private mileage. On the other hand, it may be easier to accept the tax charge because it could be less than you would actually have to pay your employer for the private mileage.

38 Own your own car rather than using your employer's

The tax payable on car benefits is now so high that it can often be cheaper to own your own car and use it for your employer's business. You would need to work it out and we certainly know of cases where, while the tax is high, the employee would rather suffer the tax than have to pay for all the outgoings that having one's own car entail. However, as we say, with the tax being high, it is quite likely that you would be better off if you owned your own car than paid the taxes that driving an employer's business car attracts.

CHAPTER 8

For those running their own business

39. Travelling expenses

40. Limited companies

41. Introduce goodwill to create a large director's loan account and pay very little tax

42. Don't automatically reclaim VAT on petrol

43. The flat-rate VAT scheme

44. National Insurance

45. Claiming 100 per cent capital allowances

46. The tax advantages of converting commercial property into residential use

47. The benefit of short-life assets

48. Use your business's losses

49. Have you claimed for all your business expenses?

50. Farmers and averaging

51. Partnerships

52. Claiming tax relief on interest

39 Travelling expenses

Expenses	Employer	Self-employed	Can VAT (input tax) be reclaimed?
	Where expenses are incurred by the employer	Where a self-employed trader incurs these expenses	
Entertaining own staff	Allowable	Allowable	Allowable**
Business travel between place of business and customers, etc. (but not home)	Allowable	Allowable	If charged, allowable
Hotel bills, etc.	Allowable	Allowable	Allowable, so long as it is billed to the VAT registered trader
Drinks and meals away from home:			
1. Working/selling	Allowable	Not allowable	Allowable**
2. On training course	Allowable	Allowable	Allowable**
3. Buying, etc. trips	Allowable	Allowable	Allowable**
*Entertaining business clients:**	Not allowable	Not allowable	Not allowable
Car parking	Allowable	Allowable	Allowable
Phone calls home	Allowable	Allowable	Allowable
Trade show expenses	Allowable	Allowable	Allowable
Petrol	Allowable	Allowable – business proportion only	Allowable***

* But a hotelier, restaurateur or someone who entertains in the normal course of his trade may claim these.

** But not if there is any measurable degree of business entertainment.

*** But if the input VAT is reclaimed, remember to include the scale charge in your OUTPUT TAX on the VAT Return.

40 Limited companies

As a private individual, your highest rate of Income Tax is 40 per cent and that starts when your taxable income reaches £31,400. On top of the Income Tax bill, there is Class 4 National Insurance to add to it.

However, for a company the highest rate of Corporation Tax is 30 per cent and that only starts when your taxable profits are over £300,000. There are a number of rates before you get that rate, but the effective rate below it is usually 19 per cent.

If you and your spouse have a business and the profits are £100,000, if we ignore personal allowances, here is how the sums work out:

Self-employment/Partnership				**Tax, etc. payable**	
Profits	100,000				
		Husband	*Wife*		
Profits Shared		50,000	50,000		
Income Tax					
2,090	10%	209	209		
30,310	22%	6,668	6,668		
17,600	40%	7,040	7,040		
50,000		13,917	13,917	27,834	
Class 4 National Insurance					
4,895	0%	0	0		
27,865	8%	2,229	2,229		
17,240	1%	172	172		
50,000		2,401	2,401	4,802	
Total tax and National Insurance payable				**32,636**	
The money the Chancellor allows you to keep				67,364	67%
Company		**Corporation Tax**			
Profits	100,000	19%	19,000	19,000	
The money the Chancellor allows the company to keep				81,000	81%

In other words, the tax saved by trading through a limited company appears to be over £13,500.

However, it's not quite as simple as that (it never is!) because if you have paid yourself a salary from the company, then you will have suffered the higher personal rates of tax, and the company and you will both have suffered National Insurance contributions. On the other hand and in addition, you may have paid yourself a dividend, which can be a very tax efficient way of getting paid.

So it is all quite complicated and professional advice must be sought. But if these figures relate in any way to what you are doing, you should discuss this with your accountant – there could be a large tax saving to be made.

41 Introduce goodwill to create a large director's loan account and pay very little tax

This should not be entered into lightly nor without professional help, but, with careful planning, if you incorporate an existing business (i.e. turn it into a limited company), you should be able to create a sum for goodwill. We don't want to confuse you with science here, but, if you introduce a sum for goodwill from your present business as you incorporate (and this really only works if there is no sum already in the balance sheet), as the business proprietor you will have created a sum in the company's balance sheet – a sum that is due back to you.

It may make more sense if we give you an example:

Let's say you have a business and it's making profits of £40,000. Now you could follow the general rule and say that a business is worth three times its profits – so this might make your business worth £120,000. But there may already be assets in your business worth £90,000, which could be cash, buildings, equipment, etc. If they are already in the business, then it would not be unreasonable to say that the value of goodwill in your business is £30,000 (i.e. the difference between what the business is worth and the assets already in it).

So you put a value of £30,000 on goodwill and the company now owes you £30,000 for this goodwill. You are then in a position to draw £30,000 out of your business tax free – when the cash-flow allows you.

One thing to beware of is that you may be caught for Capital Gains Tax for handing a valuable sum for goodwill to a company. But, if you have no other gains in the year concerned, it is very unlikely that you would pay any Capital Gains Tax on transferring this sum into your company.

As we say, you will need professional advice over this but it is a very useful way of drawing tax-free cash from a business.

42 Don't automatically reclaim VAT on petrol

It is not always a good idea to claim input tax (i.e. the VAT you have to pay) on petrol.

The rule over claiming input tax on your petrol purchases is that if you claim VAT on your petrol purchases, you have to add the petrol fuel scale charge to your output tax (i.e. the VAT you charge your customers) – you will find the figures for the fuel scale charge in the Appendix. What this can mean (and is the usual case) is that you can end up paying Customs and Excise more than you are claiming back from it and this may not easily be worth your while. The only person who can work out whether it is worth your while is you.

43 The flat-rate VAT scheme

Are you registered for VAT but hate the complexity of VAT returns? Provided your turnover is less than £150,000 per annum, then it is possible to request that the flat-rate scheme applies. The payment due to Customs and Excise is a percentage of your standard-rated turnover, so you do not have to calculate your input VAT every quarter. The exact percentage applied is determined by the nature of your business activity and full details are available on the Customs and Excise website. Switching to this scheme could save you time and money, but you would have to look at each case on its own merits. If you usually have a large amount of input VAT, then the scheme may not be suitable for you.

44 National Insurance

While most of the ideas for reducing your tax bill in this book involve larger sums of tax saving, this one concerns one of the smallest figures of savings on offer, if not the smallest.

If you are just starting out in business, you are unlikely to make large profits in your first year of trading. This is not guaranteed to happen but it usually turns out this way.

Now you have to register your business with both the Inland Revenue and the National Insurance office and the latter will demand that, as a self-employed person, you pay (what used to be called) the weekly stamp of £2.10. Such a sum is unlikely to break the bank but you can get into trouble if you don't pay it.

However, if your profits are to be under £4,345 (2005/06 figure), you can claim exemption from paying it. Do remember that opting out may affect your entitlement to state pension, Maternity Benefit, Incapacity Benefit and Bereavement Allowance. The current rate is only £2.10 per week, which we think is a small price to pay for maintaining your National Insurance record.

45 Claiming 100 per cent capital allowances

A business can claim 100 per cent first-year allowances (i.e. you can effectively write off all the capital costs against your trading profit) if it incurs qualifying expenditure on designated energy-saving plant and machinery. There are currently 16 categories including such things as lighting, heating, refrigeration, motors and variable speed drives.

There are also 100 per cent allowances on water efficient equipment (e.g. flushes, taps, leakage detection equipment and flow control equipment).

If you are considering purchasing plant or equipment that is in the specified categories, then to buy the energy efficient option will (a) give you full tax relief immediately, (b) probably reduce your long-term running costs and (c) help save the planet.

Before spending your money, visit the Enhanced Capital Allowances website at www.eca.gov.uk. This list is constantly being updated so do check it regularly.

46 The tax advantages of converting commercial property into residential use

If you have a shop or other commercial premises with vacant or underused premises above, capital allowances can be claimed on converting this space into residential flats. The capital allowances are treated as expenditure when calculating the letting profit or loss. An initial allowance of 100 per cent is available if desired. While there may be a balancing adjustment needed if the property is sold within seven years of the flat being available to let, there is no adjustment for disposals after that time.

To qualify, the properties must have been built before 1980, the ground floor must be rated for business use, there must be no more than four upper storeys, they must have been empty or used for storage for at least a year and the new development must not have more than four rooms, excluding bathroom and kitchen. There are also income limits in respect of the rental value of the flats. This list of issues is not meant to be exhaustive and the matter should be fully researched with the Inland Revenue before embarking on the project so that you know whether or not the project will qualify for this relief.

47 The benefit of short-life assets

Items of plant and equipment that have a short life (typically four years or less) should be placed in a short-life assets pool. This will allow a balancing allowance or charge to arise if the asset is disposed of within four years. An election for this to apply to items purchased has to be made within one year after 31 January following the tax year in which the period of accounts ends in which the purchase was made.

Failure to make an election (which is irrevocable) will mean that the balancing adjustment for the disposal will only be made when the business ceases.

48 Use your business's losses

If you have made a loss in your business, look carefully at how best those losses can be utilised. Losses can be set against your general income for the year that they arise and/or the previous year. Also, the losses can be carried forward to set against future profits of the same trade.

In a new business the losses may also be carried back and set against general income of the previous three years, the earliest first.

A loss on cessation can be relieved against trading income of the final year and/or against trading income of the three previous years, latest first.

Ensure that you get relief not only against tax for the losses, but also against your Class 4 National Insurance contributions liability.

A loss claim can be extended to include relief against capital gains in the year of the loss and/or the previous year.

Loss-relief claims can be quite complex, particularly if there are multiple claims. It is vital that the implications of the claims are carefully reviewed and, if necessary, professional advice taken.

49 Have you claimed for all your business expenses?

See the template on the following page.

50 Farmers and averaging

Farmers and market gardeners, whether trading on their own or in partnership, may average their profits over two tax years if the profit of one year is less than 70 per cent of the profit of the other year. If the profit is between 70 per cent and 75 per cent relative to the other, then there is a marginal relief available.

The purpose of this treatment is to smooth out the peaks and troughs of good and bad years. You could, for instance, be paying higher-rate tax in one year and nothing in the following year. An averaging claim, while a little complex, can be very worthwhile, as it optimises the use of personal allowances, capital allowances and agricultural building allowances. This not only minimises your tax liabilities, but also it can maximise your entitlements to tax credits and the like.

An averaging claim must be made within a year of 31 January following the end of the second tax year, and a claim cannot be made in the first or last year of trading. The averaging can continue year after year.

A template to help you prepare your figures for the self-employed part of the Tax Return

Your name ______________________ Accounting year end ______________________

Self-Employment and Partnerships

Sales income		[ ]	A
less **Costs of sales,** e.g. raw materials and stocks	[ ]		
Construction industry subcontractors' costs	[ ]		
Other direct costs, e.g. packing and despatch	[ ]		
Total cost of sales		[ ]	B
Gross profit or loss A – B		[ ]	C
Other income		[ ]	D
Expenditure			
Employee costs Salaries, wages, bonuses, employer's NIC, pension contributions, casual wages, canteen costs, recruitment agency fees, subcontractors' (unless shown above) and other wages costs	[ ]		
Premises costs Rent, ground rent, rates, water, refuse, light and heat, property insurance, security and use of home	[ ]		
Repairs Repair of property, replacements, renewals, maintenance	[ ]		
General administrative expenses Telephone, fax, mobile telephone, stationery, photocopying, printing, postage, courier and computer costs, subscriptions, insurance	[ ]		
Motoring expenses Petrol, servicing, licence, repairs, motor insurance, hire and leasing, car parking, RAC/AA membership	[ ]		
Travel and subsistence Rail, air, bus, etc., travel, taxis, subsistence and hotel costs	[ ]		
Entertainment Staff entertaining (e.g. Christmas party), customer gifts up to £50 per person advertising your business	[ ]		
Advertising and promotion Advertising, promotion, mailshots, free samples, brochures, newsletters, trade shows, etc.	[ ]		
Legal and professional costs Accountancy, legal, architects, surveyors, stocktakers' fees, indemnity insurance	[ ]		
Bad debts (if already included in A above)	[ ]		
Interest on bank loans, overdraft and other loans	[ ]		
Other finance charges Bank charges, HP interest, credit card charges, leasing not already included	[ ]		
Depreciation and losses on sale (please ask for advice)	[ ]		
Other items – please describe	[ ]		
Grand total of expenses		[ ]	E
Net profit (or loss)	C + D – E	[ ]	

51 Partnerships

Have a proper partnership deed to prove the partnership exists and make sure there is a partnership bank account and proper letterhead for the same reason.

Partnerships can be tricky things – they are not to be entered into lightly. For one, if your partner goes bust, you could easily find that you are (what is called) 'jointly and severally liable' for each others' debts. So be very careful whom you go into partnership with.

Partnerships cannot just be set up at a whim. They need to be planned and created properly, and a number of them can save a significant sum in tax.

What are the golden rules of partnerships and what are the things you should look out for?

- The taxman may need proof that what you have created is indeed a partnership. To do this, you should be able to show him:
  - a partnership bank account (with the names of the partners or at least the name of the partnership on the statements);
  - letterheads, invoices, business cards, etc.;
  - advertisements (as in Yellow Pages) in the name of the partnership;
  - brochures, if you have them; and
  - a proper partnership deed. You really should have one of these, not just to show the taxman, but as a formal record of the terms under which you and your partner(s) agreed to go into business. If something were to go wrong (and partnerships have a habit of going wrong – partners fall out or, worse still, partners can die), it is vital to have it all recorded what the partners should do in such an eventuality.

52 Claiming tax relief on interest

If you borrow money to buy shares in a private company or a share in a partnership, or to buy plant and machinery for business use, you should be able to get tax relief on the interest at your top rate of tax. So if you are a higher-rate taxpayer, this will be 40 per cent. Similarly, if you borrow money to lend to a partnership or company, tax relief will be due providing you are not a limited partner or a partner in an investment limited liability partnership (i.e. a business that makes investments). If the loan is to a company, you must own at least five per cent of the issued share capital and also work there, more or less full time, in a managerial capacity.

CHAPTER 9

National Insurance

53. It may be advisable for a married woman to pay NI contributions, even though she doesn't have to

54. Get a state pension forecast well before retirement age

55. Don't pay too much National Insurance

53 It may be advisable for a married woman to pay NI contributions, even though she doesn't have to

If you are a married woman who elected to pay reduced-rate contributions, it may be advisable to withdraw this election to increase the amount of your state pension.

54 Get a state pension forecast well before retirement age

If you don't qualify for the full amount, you may be able to boost your entitlement. The forecast can be obtained by filling out Form BR19, available online at www.thepensionservice.gov.uk or by phoning 0845 3000 168.

55 Don't pay too much National Insurance

If you are employed as well as self-employed, you may be paying too much National Insurance. Consider deferring Class 2 and/or Class 4 contributions and the Inland Revenue will then check the position after the end of the tax year.

CHAPTER 10
Capital Gains Tax

56. Make use of the annual Capital Gains Tax exemption (1)

57. Make use of the annual Capital Gains Tax exemption (2)

58. Don't overlook claiming relief for shares that are now worthless

59. Taper relief

60. Assets you can sell without incurring Capital Gains Tax

61. Suggestions for investments with tax advantages

62. It can be a good idea to crystallise capital gains if there is going to be no tax to pay

63. Claim rollover relief

64. Time your sales to defer payment of Capital Gains Tax

65. Reduce or eliminate Capital Gains Tax on a second home

56 Make use of the annual Capital Gains Tax exemption (1)

In 2005/06 the Capital Gains Tax annual exemption is £8,500. If you can structure your financial affairs to give you gains each year that do not exceed this figure, you effectively have extra tax-free income. Investments giving rise to gains are most frequently unit trusts and shares, although those held in ISAs and investments in government gilts do not have any capital gains liability.

While most people accept that investments of this type can go down as well as up, if you make investments through an authorised adviser and you suffer a loss because of poor advice, poor investment management or the adviser going out of business, there is a Financial Services Compensation Scheme, which can pay compensation of up to £48,000 – for more information, visit its website at www.fscs.org.uk.

57 Make use of the annual Capital Gains Tax exemption (2)

Assets transferred between spouses are exempt and each spouse is entitled to the exempt amount of £8,500 (2005/06 figure).

If there will be tax to pay, consider transferring the asset to the non-taxpaying (or lower-rate taxpaying) spouse. But a word of caution: if this is a business asset, you should seek professional advice first as you may lose out on the valuable business taper relief (see number 59).

Transfers between spouses followed by a sale could be attacked by the Revenue as an anti-avoidance measure, so there should be a delay between the transfer and the subsequent sale. There should be no strings attached to the gift whatsoever, particularly something which might result in the eventual proceeds going back to the transferor.

58 Don't overlook claiming relief for shares that are now worthless

If you have tax to pay, check to see if you or your spouse have shares in companies that are now worthless. If you do, whatever those shares cost will equal a loss which can be offset against gains. Remember to transfer the shares to the spouse who has the gain first.

59 Taper relief

Taper relief works by taxing only a percentage of the gain depending on the number of years you have held the asset and whether the asset is a business or non-business asset. The maximum relief for business assets after two years is 75 per cent, leaving only 25 per cent chargeable. For non-business assets the maximum rate is 60 per cent, leaving 40 per cent taxable, but only after ten years. (See the table on the following page.) Assets qualifying as business assets are:

- Assets used for the purposes of a trade carried on by an individual either on his own or in partnership, or assets used by a qualifying company.
- Assets held that are used for your employment, providing it is a trading company and you work there more or less full time.
- Shares that you hold in a qualifying company which includes shares held on the Alternative Investment Market.

Assets falling under the first point include property used for furnished holiday lettings and also property used by either a trading company or an unincorporated business, but not properties used for other types of letting. To qualify as furnished holiday letting, the property must:

- be available as holiday accommodation for at least 140 days in a tax year; and
- be let on a commercial basis for at least 70 days; and

Capital Gains Tax taper relief

Gains on disposal of business assets		Gains on disposals of non-business assets	
No. of whole years in qualifying holding period	Percentage of gain chargeable	No. of whole years in qualifying holding period	Percentage of gain chargeable
0	100	0	100
1	87.5	1	100
2	75	2	100
3	50	3	95
4	25	4	90
5	25	5	85
6	25	6	80
7	25	7	75
8	25	8	70
9	25	9	65
10 or more	25	10 or more	60

- not be occupied for more than 31 days by the same person in any period of seven months.

Since the introduction of taper relief, the definition of what constitutes a business asset has changed several times. If there has been mixed usage during ownership, the gain has to be apportioned and this will be based on definitions applying at the time of usage and not at the time of sale. It is a complex area so professional advice should be taken.

60 Assets you can sell without incurring Capital Gains Tax

You can sell chattels such as jewellery, pictures and furniture where the proceeds are £6,000 or less without incurring Capital Gains Tax. Please note that if you sell, say, a set of chairs for more than £6,000, you cannot claim this as being free from Capital Gains Tax on the basis that each individual chair was sold for less than £6,000. The Inland Revenue looks at the set as being the item, not the individual items themselves. These include:

- Compensation for damages

- Decorations for gallantry unless you bought them in the first place
- Foreign currency
- Gifts of outstanding public interest that are given to the nation
- Gifts to charities
- Government stocks
- Your own house
- ISAs
- Land and buildings given to the National Trust
- Life policies and deferred annuities
- Motor cars, including veteran and vintage models*
- Guns*
- Wine*
- Antique clocks and watches*
- Premium bonds
- Personal equity plans (PEPs)
- Save As You Earn schemes
- Shares subscribed under the business expansion scheme or an Enterprise Investment Scheme

*Providing that they are not used in a business.

61 Suggestions for investments with tax advantages

While it is not our business to suggest individual investments, the following investments have certain tax advantages:

- **National Savings Certificates**
- **Children's bonus bonds:** these are high-interest savings schemes for children under the age of 16. You can buy the bonds at any post office and both the interest and the bonus are tax free.

- **Enterprise Investment Scheme:** if you invest in this, Income Tax relief is given at 20 per cent up to £200,000 invested in any year. The gains are free of Capital Gains Tax, but there is neither Income Tax relief nor Capital Gains Tax relief for any losses when you sell these shares. The shares must be held for at least three years. There are other rules concerning the Enterprise Investment Scheme but I think this covers the most important ones.
- **Venture Capital Trusts:** investors are exempt from tax on dividends so long as the shares purchased did not cost more than £200,000 – the rate set in April 2004. If you subscribe for up to £200,000 worth of shares, you get up to 40 per cent tax relief but you have to hold onto the shares for three years.

62 It can be a good idea to crystallise capital gains if there is going to be no tax to pay

Each year you are entitled to make tax-free capital gains of £8,500 (2005/06 figure). If you have not made any gains and have (say) some shares that, if you were to sell them, would achieve a taxable gain of no more than £8,500, it would make sense to sell them and then buy them back (if you wanted to keep the shares) because you would then have them at a higher cost of acquisition and if you were to sell them again in the future, this would reduce or possibly eliminate any taxable gain when that happens. If you do buy the shares back, you have to wait for 30 days to do so.

63 Claim rollover relief

If you make a gain on the sale of a qualifying business asset, and reinvest the proceeds in a new qualifying business asset, within the period starting one year before and ending three years after the original disposal, a claim may be made to have the gain deferred.

Qualifying business assets include land and buildings (including property which qualifies as furnished holiday lettings); plant and machinery; ships;

aircrafts; hovercrafts; goodwill; milk, potato and fish quotas; ewe and suckler cow premium quotas and Lloyds syndicate rights.

For the very adventurous business person, satellites, spacestations and spacecrafts are also included!

The replacement asset does not have to be within the same category as the asset sold.

Where only some of the sale proceeds are reinvested, the remaining part of the gain is immediately chargeable.

64 Time your sales to defer payment of Capital Gains Tax

A tax deferred gives you a cash-flow advantage, so it makes sense to delay the due date for paying tax whenever you can. If you sell an asset on 5 April, you will have to pay the Capital Gains Tax nine months later. If you delay the sale by just one day and sell on 6 April, the Capital Gains Tax does not have to be paid for 22 months. Don't forget the date of sale for Capital Gains Tax purposes is the date you exchange contracts and not the completion date.

65 Reduce or eliminate Capital Gains Tax on a second home

If you are about to purchase or have purchased a second home, you can elect (within two years from buying the second one) which is to be the principal family home for Capital Gains Tax purposes. This is a complex area and it is recommended that you take professional advice.

A further consideration worth looking into would be if you are selling a second home and there is tax to pay, could you occupy it for a short time as your main residence as this may reduce the tax payable?

CHAPTER 11

Inheritance Tax

66 Check up to see what your Inheritance Tax is likely to be

I own	**Estimated value**	**At my death I would like to leave this to:**
House		
Valuables		
Shares		
Cash		
Other land and property		
Trust		
Business assets		
The residue of my estate		
Legacies I would like to give		Details:
Substantial gifts I have made in the last seven years		Gifted to:
Less Sums I owe	( )	How will these be repaid on death?
Total estate		
Less tax-free band	**(275,000)**	
Total net		
Tax due @ 40%		

67 What gifts are exempt from Inheritance Tax?

Many gifts are exempt from tax so make use of these exemptions.

- Gifts between spouses, but if one spouse is not UK domiciled, the lifetime exemption is limited to £55,000.
- Gifts of up to £3,000 in each tax year are exempt and the unused portion of the previous year's exemption can be carried forward but only for one year.
- A gift of £250 to any one person if the total gifts to that person do not exceed £250. This can be used to cover Christmas and birthday gifts from grandparents to grandchildren.
- Wedding gifts of up to:
    - £5,000 from each parent to each child;
    - £2,500 from each grandparent;
    - £1,000 from anybody else.

  The gift must be made shortly before the marriage and becomes effective when the marriage takes place.
- If you have surplus income year on year, this can be gifted free of Inheritance Tax. You need to be able to show that such gifts are part of your regular annual income expenditure and do not reduce your standard of living. The exemption can be used if you pay life insurance premiums for the benefit of someone else. You should keep a record of these gifts and if possible a record of your net (after tax) income. This can be a very useful exemption as there is no upper limit so it is worth keeping the documentation.
- Gifts to UK charities, political parties (providing they have at least one MP and 150,000 votes), registered housing associations and gifts for national purposes are also exempt.
- Maintenance payments to your dependants and ex-spouse.

If the gift is not covered by any of these exemptions, then providing you survive for seven years it will be free of Inheritance Tax.

68 Inheritance Tax business/agricultural property relief

Certain categories of business and business assets may qualify for 100 per cent exemption from Inheritance Tax after two years. The relief normally applies to a business or an interest in a business (partnership) or to shares in an unlisted company. Shares quoted on the Alternative Investment Market also qualify after two years. The exemption also applies to farmers after two years if they farm the land and after seven years if the farm is let to someone else who farms the land. Full details of these reliefs are beyond the scope of this book and professional advice should be taken.

69 Don't leave everything to your wife – use the tax-free band carefully

This is one of those matters that are obvious when they are explained but not so obvious previously. Let's say that you have assets worth £1 million and in your Will you leave everything to your wife. No Inheritance Tax will be paid on your death (assuming you die first), but on hers, nearly £750,000 will bear tax at 40 per cent, resulting in your children paying almost £300,000 on her death.

But if your wife has enough to live on if you were to give your tax-free band to your children and not to her, no tax would be paid on your death (no change there) but on her death, her taxable estate would be about £500,000 and the tax due on that amount would be approximately £200,000. Therefore, by this judicious use of your Will, you would save your children approximately £100,000.

CHAPTER 12

Overseas aspects

70 Can you save tax by going abroad?

Residence, domicile, etc.

The overseas aspects of UK taxation is a complex area, but, in general terms, if you are a UK resident, you will be liable to UK tax on your world income. If you are not a UK resident, you will only be liable to pay UK tax on income arising in the UK.

Without wanting to make matters too complex, reference will be made to the terms residence, ordinary residence and domicile.

Residence

You will always be a UK resident if you spend 183 days per year in the UK excluding the days of arrival and departure. Being in the UK for less than 183 days per year does **not** automatically mean that you are not resident. It is possible to be resident in more than one country at a time.

Ordinary residence

If you are generally resident in the UK year after year, even though on occasion you may not be resident for a particular tax year, then you are ordinarily resident.

Domicile

A person's domicile is usually the country in which he has his permanent home and other related connections. When you are born you usually take your father's domicile ('domicile of origin'). Until you are able to change it, you will follow the domicile of the person on whom you are dependent ('domicile of dependency'). It is also possible to change your domicile by moving to another country and thoroughly embedding yourself within the society and culture ('domicile of choice'). There are high standards of proof for this, however.

The domicile of married women is now determined independently of their husbands.

Leaving the UK

Strictly speaking, you are resident or not resident for a complete tax year. By concession you can split your year of departure into resident up to the date of departure and non-resident from that date. When leaving the UK you should complete Form P85 and if it is your intention to be abroad for at least one complete tax year, you will be treated as provisionally non-resident. You must not be in the UK for more than 183 days in any year and the average number of days in the UK over the period of your absence must not exceed 91 days per year. Periods spent in the UK for exceptional reasons (e.g. serious illness) are usually ignored.

Providing you establish and maintain your non-resident status, any earnings abroad of a UK domiciled person will not be liable to UK Income Tax.

There are, however, special rules for Crown employees (e.g. civil servants, diplomats, members of the armed forces, etc.) and these people should refer to the Inland Revenue for clarification of their position.

There are special rules relating to seafarers and aircrew. There may be eligibility for a Foreign Earnings Deduction, but this matter should be explored with the Inland Revenue.

Arriving in the UK

If you arrive in the UK, you are treated as resident and ordinarily resident from your date of arrival if you intend to live here permanently or actually remain here for more than three complete tax years. Form P86 should be completed and submitted to the Inland Revenue. Issues of what you intend and subsequently what you actually do in terms of the time spent in the UK are both very important. Matters will be reviewed each year and after four years it will be possible to decide definitely what an individual's residence status is. Being treated as resident and ordinarily resident will bring an entitlement to UK personal allowances – see the Appendix.

Non-residents cannot claim UK personal allowances unless they are UK, Commonwealth or Republic of Ireland citizens or EEA nationals (EU countries plus Iceland, Norway and Liechtenstein).

If you are UK resident and domiciled and in receipt of a pension from overseas, you can claim a ten per cent deduction on the amount of pension liable to tax in the UK.

People becoming non-resident in the UK but retaining a property here which is going to be let out become non-resident landlords. The Inland Revenue needs to be notified on Form NRL1. The Inland Revenue can authorise the rents to be paid without the deduction of basic-rate tax, by the letting agent or the tenant, which is what should happen automatically. Provided the landlord is within one of the categories above, a claim for UK personal allowances can be made to minimise tax liabilities.

Non-residents who are in receipt of the UK state pension can disclaim personal allowances and have the full amount of state pension removed from their tax liability calculations.

If an individual left the UK after 17 March 1998 and has been non-resident for five complete tax years from the date of departure, there is no liability to Capital Gains Tax on assets sold prior to his return to the UK.

If you are resident but not domiciled in the UK, or resident but not ordinarily resident in the UK and a Commonwealth citizen (includes UK) or a citizen of the Republic of Ireland, you will be taxed on income remitted to the UK (i.e. paid to the UK). Where the remittance basis applies you are liable to UK tax on all overseas income that is paid into or brought into the UK in any way. If you are subject to the remittance basis, you should have the interest derived from foreign savings paid into a separate account, i.e. do not allow the interest to accrue in the same account as the capital on which it is accruing. This is because if it is the same account, there is a danger that you will pay tax on the capital when the money is remitted.

Queries on overseas and residence issues are best directed to the Inland Revenue at the Centre for Non-Residents, Residence Advice and Liabilities (Unit 355), St Johns House, Merton Road, Bootle, Merseyside L69 9BB; tel. 0845 070 0040.

Scope of liability to Income Tax of earnings

		Duties of Employment Performed Wholly or Partly in the UK		Duties of Employment Performed Wholly Outside the UK
		In the UK	*Outside the UK*	
Foreign Emoluments[1]	Employee resident and ordinarily resident in the UK	Liable – less possible deduction[2]	Liable – less possible deduction[2]	Liable if received in the UK[3]
	Resident but not ordinarily resident	Liable	Liable if received in the UK[3]	Liable if received in the UK[3]
	Not resident	Liable	Not liable	Not liable
Other Earnings	Resident and ordinarily resident	Liable – less possible deduction[2]	Liable – less possible deduction[2]	Liable – less possible deduction[2]
	Resident but not ordinarily resident	Liable	Liable if received in the UK[3]	Liable if received in the UK[3]
	Not resident	Liable	Not liable	Not liable

1. 'Foreign emoluments' is the term used in the Taxes Act to mean the earnings of someone who is not domiciled in the UK and whose employer is resident outside, and not resident in, the UK (nor resident in the Republic of Ireland).

2. There may be a foreign earnings deduction of 100 per cent in these cases from the amount chargeable, if the earnings are for a period which is part of a qualifying absence lasting 365 days or more – this means that such earnings for that period will be free from UK tax. This generally only applies to seafarers.

3. The remittance basis which applies in these cases.

Scope of liability to Income Tax on individuals receiving pensions

	Paid by or on Behalf of a Person	
	In the UK	*Outside the UK (Overseas Pension)*
Residence Status and Domicile		
Resident and ordinarily resident, and domiciled	Liable	Liable[1]
Resident and ordinarily resident, not domiciled	Liable	Liable if received in the UK[2]
Resident but not ordinarily resident, domiciled	Liable	Liable[1,3]
Resident but not ordinarily resident, not domiciled	Liable	Liable if received in the UK[2]
Not resident	Liable[4,5]	Not liable

1. Less than ten per cent deduction.
2. You are taxable on the whole of a pension arising in the Republic of Ireland, less ten per cent deduction; but if the pension is from the Irish Government, you are taxable only if you are a UK national without also being an Irish national.
3. If you are a Commonwealth (this includes British) citizen or an Irish citizen, the remittance basis applies and the ten per cent deduction is not due, unless the pension arises in the Irish Republic, in which case note 2 applies.
4. There may be relief under a double taxation agreement.
5. It may be beneficial not to claim UK personal allowances.

Scope of liability to Income Tax on profits of individuals carrying on a trade or profession

	Trade or Profession Carried on Wholly or Partly in the UK	Trade or Profession Carried on Wholly Outside the UK
Residence Status and Domicile		
Resident and ordinarily resident, and domiciled	Liable	Liable
Resident and ordinarily resident, not domiciled	Liable	Liable if received in the UK[1]
Resident but not ordinarily resident, domiciled	Liable	Liable[2]
Resident but not ordinarily resident, not domiciled	Liable	Liable if received in the UK[1]
Not resident	Liable[3]	Not liable

1. You are taxable on the whole of the income from a trade or profession carried on wholly in the Republic of Ireland.
2. If you are a Commonwealth (this includes British) citizen or an Irish citizen, the remittance basis applies unless the trade or profession is carried on wholly in the Irish Republic, in which case note 1 applies.
3. You are liable on the profits of the part of the trade or profession carried on in the UK.

CHAPTER 13

When someone dies

71 Don't overpay Inheritance Tax on assets that are sold

Inheritance Tax is a very damaging tax. Not only are the rates very high (they start at 40 per cent) and the sums payable tend to have a great many noughts after them, but, on top of this, the tax has to be paid from a bank account that probably has no cash in it with which to pay the tax. It is what can be called an 'ouch'.

There are few ameliorations of this dreadful state of affairs but there is one and it is often overlooked.

Inheritance Tax is paid on the probate value of the assets. This is the professional value that is put on the assets when the tax is calculated. But if you sell certain of these assets within either four years of death for land and property (one year for quoted securities) and they realise a sum that is lower than probate, you can apply to the Capital Taxes Office for a refund of 40 per cent of the difference between the two. You can only get the relief if there is an overall loss on quoted securities. The relief is not due solely on the shares that have fallen in value.

While on this subject, if the asset is sold for a higher sum, then remember that Capital Gains Tax may be payable.

72 Remember to claim full probate costs when someone dies

When an inherited asset is to be sold, the cost will be its probate value. This can be increased further to make some allowance for probate costs. The amount allowed is based on the size of the estate and ranges from 1.75 per cent if the estate is valued at up to £40,000 to 0.75 per cent for estates valued between £400,000 and £750,000. If the value exceeds £750,000, the allowable costs are negotiable.

73 Capital Gains Tax and Inheritance Tax considerations

If elderly people are considering giving away their assets to reduce Inheritance Tax, bear in mind that there is no Capital Gains Tax to pay on death and the beneficiaries will inherit assets at probate value. This could be considerably higher than the value at the time of the gift so the beneficiaries may be able to sell the asset after death without incurring Capital Gains Tax. This needs careful planning as you could end up paying more Inheritance Tax than the Capital Gains Tax saved.

While on this subject, estates of deceased persons enjoy Capital Gains Tax annual exemption for two years after death.

If an asset that belonged to someone who has died is sold within (roughly) two years of his death, there could be Capital Gains Tax due on the sale proceeds, but estates of deceased persons can claim the annual exemption for not only the tax year in which they died but the following two years as well.

CHAPTER 14

Pensions

74 Take out a pension

If you contribute to a pension scheme, the government will add a further £2.80 for every £10 you pay and if you are a higher-rate taxpayer, the government contribution increases to £6.66. And don't forget, once the money is invested it grows in a tax-free environment with one exception. Unfortunately, the government will no longer repay the ten per cent tax credit attached to dividends paid to your accumulating fund.

75 You may be able to take out a pension even if you are not earning

Stakeholder pensions are not just for workers. Non-earning spouses and children can have a stakeholder. So for higher-rate taxpayers, this is a useful way of sheltering your capital from Income Tax and investing it in a tax-free environment for the benefit of your family.

CHAPTER 15

Property

76. Rent a room

77. VAT and rent

78. Income from property

79. Have you claimed for all the expenses you can?

80. Claim the interest on any loan you take out to buy the property

81. Do you and your wife jointly own the property?

82. Forestry

76 Rent a room

You can receive gross rents of up to £4,250 tax free per year for letting furnished rooms in your own home. If you own two properties, the relief only applies to the main family home. If the property is jointly owned, the relief is divided between you. Should the rent you receive exceed this amount, you have two choices. You can choose to pay tax on the excess over £4,250 or on the rent you receive less the expenses. You have to make a claim if you want to pay on the excess over £4,250 and this basis will apply until you withdraw the claim. This relief is usually used when people take in lodgers so it won't apply if the rooms you let comprise of a flat with its own facilities. If the rent is within the rent-a-room scheme, there won't be any Capital Gains Tax issues if you ever sell your house.

The relief is not just for owner-occupiers. If you are a tenant in rented accommodation, you will also qualify if you sublet a room, providing that it is your main home.

It is advisable to tell your mortgage company and your insurers if you enter into a rent-a-room arrangement.

77 VAT and rent

If you are VAT registered and you also have rental income, you are making what the VAT man calls 'exempt' as well as 'zero-rated' supplies. You cannot charge VAT on the rent and equally you cannot reclaim VAT on the rent expenses. Normally, a partly exempt business has to use a special method to work out how much VAT it can reclaim. However, if the input tax in any VAT period is not more than:

1. £625 per month on average; and
2. one half of all input tax for the period concerned;

all the input tax on the rent expenses can be reclaimed.

Obviously, the above does not apply if you receive rent from non-domestic property and you have chosen to tax these rents.

78 Income from property

If you buy commercial property to let out, you can claim business asset taper relief.

With the arrival of business asset taper relief, which is a much more attractive relief than non-business asset taper relief, the more assets you can put into this category, the better. So remember that while most property purchases do not attract business asset taper relief (so property sales tend to attract the payment of large sums in Capital Gains Tax) any property that does attract this relief will pay far less than otherwise. Properties of this nature include commercial properties and those acquired for furnished holiday lettings.

79 Have you claimed for all the expenses you can?

See the template on the following page.

80 Claim the interest on any loan you take out to buy the property

If you borrow money to buy a property to let, you will get tax relief on the interest you pay at your top rate of tax. You can also get tax relief on loans to fund improvements, alterations or repairs.

There is an interesting addition to the Inland Revenue manuals which indicates that interest on funds borrowed for private purposes may be deductible against rental income in certain circumstances. This has wide-reaching implications for buy-to-let investors.

One example in the manual covers Mr A, who owns a flat in London and is moving abroad. He decides to let the property while he is away. During his period of ownership, the property has trebled in value. He renegotiates the mortgage to convert it to a buy-to-let mortgage and borrows a further amount which he uses to buy a property overseas. Can he claim tax relief

A template to help you prepare your figures for the land and property income part of the Tax Return

Your name ______________________________

Land and Property Income (year to 5 April)

Income

Received from	Rents received £
Total income	£
Tax already deducted from property income	£

Expenditure

	£	£
Premises Rents		
Rates		
Property insurance		
Light and heat		
Cleaning		
Security		
Subtotal		
Repairs and maintenance Repairs and renewals		
Redecorating		
Small tools		
Subtotal		
Finance charges and interest on loan to buy rented property		
Legal and professional Legal		
Accountancy		
Debt collection		
Other insurances		
Subscriptions		
Architects' fees		
Subtotal		
Services provided Wages		
Telephone		
TV		
Garden		
Roads		
Subtotal		
Other costs Advertising		
Agents' fees		
Office costs		
Travel		
Subtotal		
Total expenditure		£

on the interest against the rents? Well, the Inland Revenue says that owners of businesses (and renting property is a business for tax purposes) are entitled to withdraw their capital from the business, even though substitute funding then has to be provided by interest-bearing loans. In the case of Mr A, his opening balance sheet shows the following:

Original mortgage	80,000	**Property at market value**	375,000
Capital account	295,000		
	375,000		375,000

When Mr A renegotiates his mortgage, he borrows a further £125,000, which goes through his property business. He then withdraws this amount to fund the purchase of the property overseas. By the end of the first year of letting, his balance sheet shows the following.

Mortgage	205,000	**Property at market value**	375,000
Capital account b/f	295,000		
Less drawings	(125,000)		
Carry forward	170,000		
	375,000		375,000

Although he has withdrawn capital from the business, the interest on the mortgage loan is allowable in full because it is funding the transfer of the property to the business at its open market value at the time the business started. Although the Inland Revenue's example has a further mortgage of £125,000, it seems that Mr A could withdraw a further £170,000 of tax-allowable finance. However, he should not take out more than he puts in as his capital account will be in the red (i.e. overdrawn).

The best advice is not to assume that you will automatically get tax relief but to take professional advice before you remortgage.

81 Do you and your wife jointly own the property?

If a husband and wife own a property in joint names (joint tenancy), the income and expenditure is always divided equally when filling in the Tax Return forms. However, if the ownership is owned as tenants in common and if you ask the tax office for Form 17, you can jointly declare the ownership split that actually applies and then you can enter those amounts on the Tax Returns.

82 Forestry

Forestry can be a good way to save tax. In principle, there are three main advantages:

1. There is no Inheritance Tax on forestry.
2. There is no Income Tax on forestry.
3. When it comes to forestry sales, only the land, not growing timber, attracts Capital Gains Tax.

There may not be much money in forestry, but at least there's virtually no tax either!

CHAPTER 16
Savings

83 Remember to claim back tax deducted from the deposit interest

If you are not a taxpayer, i.e. your annual taxable income is less than your personal allowances (see number 10), you can elect to have any bank or building society interest you receive to be paid without tax being deducted. In the majority of cases, and in the absence of such an election, interest is paid after 20 per cent tax has been deducted and it is 'net' interest rather than 'gross'. If you are not a taxpayer (or only liable at ten per cent) but have suffered tax on your interest, then you will be due a refund.

84 ISAs and investments

Most people will have heard of Individual Savings Accounts (ISAs), which allow interest to be paid tax free. Shares can also be held in an ISA and these can be sold free of Capital Gains Tax. There are, however, various maximum limits applicable, which are as follows:

Mini ISA: cash – £3,000; shares – £3,000; insurance policies – £1,000

Maxi ISA: shares – £7,000

There is also a range of National Savings investments available, but these can involve locking your capital away for a fixed period and there is also a maximum amount that can be invested each year. National Savings Certificates should be considered as the interest is paid tax free. Therefore, the interest rates paid can be very attractive to higher-rate taxpayers. Pensioners who would have their age-related allowances reduced by receiving taxable income should also give consideration to tax-free investments (those with taxable incomes over £19,500 in 20005/06).

85 Premium savings bonds

If you like a flutter but don't want to risk your capital, premium bonds may be for you. The minimum investment is £100 and the maximum holding is £30,000. The monthly draw results in prizes of various amounts which are tax free. You can encash the bonds at any time for face value.

CHAPTER 17

Charitable giving

86 Gift Aid

If you 'Gift Aid' a donation to charity, the charity claims back the basic-rate tax that is deemed to have been deducted from the grossed-up payment. Therefore, for every pound you Gift Aid to charity, the charity claims an additional 28p. (However, you must have paid at least 28p in tax yourself.)

In addition to feeling good about your generosity, you are also entitled to tax relief at an additional 18 per cent on your donation. This is achieved by extending your basic-rate band, i.e. more of your income is charged to tax at 22 per cent rather than 40 per cent. You can also elect for your gift to be treated as paid in the previous tax year so that higher-rate relief can be claimed in that year.

87 Charities

As well as cash gifts to charities, tax relief is also available on gifts of shares, securities (including AIM shares, unit trusts, etc.) and land and buildings. Individuals will get Income Tax relief on the market value of the gift on the date of the gift, plus any incidental costs of disposal or transfer, less any consideration or benefit received, at their top rate of tax. In addition, companies can claim relief. Such gifts to charities are exempt from Capital Gains Tax so neither a chargeable gain nor allowable loss will arise. Care is needed if the gift is a building on which capital allowances have been claimed as this is likely to result in a tax liability which would reduce the value of the tax relief otherwise due.

CHAPTER 18
Marriage and children

88 Give children assets when they are not worth very much

This is one of those points which, while obvious, often gets overlooked. Let's say that you are setting up a new business and it is to be a limited company. (This is not the only sort of opportunity to which this idea might relate but it happens to make the point very well.)

So you have just incorporated the business, it hasn't yet traded and is worth extremely little. If you were to give some shares to your children on day one and if we assume that the business does well and in a few years' time it is worth a tidy sum of money, the capital growth will all belong to the children.

If, however, you delay giving them the shares, then when you transfer them to the children, you may have to pay Capital Gains Tax on the gift.

89 What are the best investments for children?

The simplest answer is that savings accounts with building societies or banks that are in the children's names should pay the children interest gross (i.e. without tax deducted).

It is still quite permissible for children to hold shares in companies, even though the tax credits on the dividends are not refundable.

If the children do not have any investments and if the parents have surplus after-tax income of their own which they give to their children, this is usually tax free in the children's hands and if the parents are particularly wealthy, is a very useful way of transferring income to them, so that the children can accumulate a sum that can then be invested. However, once the income from the source exceeds £100 per annum, it will be taxed in the hands of the parents. If parents transfer their own shares to their children and the children are under 18, the income arising on these shares will be regarded as belonging to the parents, so this does not save tax.

90 Plan separation and divorce carefully

Assets transferred between married couples who are living together are exempt from Capital Gains Tax. This exemption also applies in the tax year in which they separate. Arranging for the division and transfer of assets can be a time-consuming process and it is not always possible to finalise this before the end of the tax year of separation, even if separation occurs very early in the tax year. When assets are transferred after the year of separation, Capital Gains Tax is charged in the normal way. This should be borne in mind when considering a matrimonial settlement.

CHAPTER 19

And finally...

91. Free Inland Revenue explanatory pamphlets – a good source of safe tax information

92. Tax planning do's

93. Tax planning don'ts

91 Free Inland Revenue explanatory pamphlets – a good source of safe tax information

The pamphlets listed are obtainable free of charge from Inland Revenue offices and Enquiry Centres, unless indicated otherwise in the text. Many, including some for which a charge is made, are available on the Inland Revenue website: www.inlandrevenue.gov.uk.

IR1	Extra-statutory concessions (2003)
IR2	Occupational pension schemes – A guide for members of tax approved schemes (2003)
IR3	Personal pension schemes (including stakeholder pension schemes) – A guide for members of tax approved schemes (2003)
IR4	Bankruptcy proceedings in England and Wales (2003)
IR5	Winding-up proceedings in England and Wales (2002)
IR8	Solicitor's Office Enforcement Section: Winding-up petitions (2002)
IR10	Paying the right tax on your earnings or pension (2004)
IR12	Practice notes on the approval of occupational pension schemes (2001 with supplement on FSAVC guidance notes)
IR14/15 (CIS)	Construction industry scheme (2003)
IR20	Residents and non-residents – Liability to tax in the UK (1999)
IR37	Appeals against tax (2003)
IR40 (CIS)	Construction industry scheme: Conditions for getting a sub-contractor's tax certificate (2003)
IR45	What to do about tax when someone dies (2001)
IR46	Clubs, societies and voluntary associations (2000)
IR56	Employed or self-employed? A guide for tax and NICs (2004)
IR59	Collection of student loans (2003)
IR60	Students and the Inland Revenue (2002)
IR64	Giving to charity by business (2004)
IR65	Giving to charity by individuals (2004)
IR68	Accrued income scheme: Taxing securities on transfer (2002)
IR69	Expenses: Payments and benefits in kind – How to save yourself work (2002)

IR76	Personal pension schemes: Guidance notes (2001)
IR78	Looking to the future. Tax reliefs to help you save for retirement (2001)
IR87	Letting your home (1999)
IR95	Approved profit sharing schemes – An outline for employees (1996)
IR97	Approved SAYE share option schemes – An outline for employees (1996)
IR98	Approved SAYE share option schemes – Explanatory notes (2002)
IR101	Approved company share option plans – An outline for employees (1996)
IR102	Approved company share option plans – Explanatory notes (1996)
IR109	Employer compliance reviews and negotiations (2002)
IR110	Bank and building society interest – A guide for savers (2003)
IR115	IT, NIC and childcare (2003)
IR116 (CIS)	A guide for subcontractors with tax certificates (2003)
IR117 (CIS)	A guide for subcontractors with registration cards (2003)
IR121	IT and pensioners (2003)
IR122	Volunteer drivers (2002)
IR124	Using your own vehicle for work (2002)
IR131	Inland Revenue Statements of Practice (2004)
IR134	IT and NIC on relocation packages (2000)
IR136	IT and company vans (2001)
IR137	The Enterprise Investment Scheme (2003)
IR138	Living or retiring abroad (1995)
IR139	Income from abroad (1995)
IR140	Non-resident landlords, their agents and tenants (2002)
IR141	Open government (2001)
IR143	IT and redundancy (2000)
IR144	IT and incapacity benefit (2002)
IR145	Low interest loans provided by employers (2001)
IR148	Construction industry: Are your workers employed or self-employed? (2001)

IR150	Taxation of rents – A guide to property income (1999)
IR152	Trusts – An introduction (2002)
IR155	PAYE settlement agreements (2001)
IR160	Inland Revenue enquiries under self-assessment (2002)
IR166	The Euro (2002)
IR167	Charter for Inland Revenue taxpayers (2003)
IR168	How tax credit settlements are negotiated (2002)
IR169	Venture Capital Trusts – A brief guide (2002)
IR170	Blind person's allowance (2003)
IR172	Income Tax and company cars (2003)
IR175	Supplying services through a limited company or partnership (2001)
IR176	Tax, NIC and green travel (2003)
IR177	Share incentive plan and your entitlement to benefits (2001)
IR178	Giving shares and securities to charity (2004)
IR179	R & D tax credits (2000)
IR180 (CIS)	A guide for non-residents (2003)
IR2000	The corporate venturing scheme (2001)
IR2001	Trading by charities (2001)
IR2002	Share incentive plan – A guide for employees (2001)
IR2003	Supplying services. How to calculate the deemed payment (2001)
IR2004	Setting up a charity in Scotland (2003). Obtainable from IR Charities, Meldrum House, 15 Drumsheugh Gardens, Edinburgh EH5 3LU (0131 777 4040)
IR2005	Share incentive plans – Guidance for employers and advisers (2001)
IR2006	Enterprise management incentives – A guide (2001)
IR2007	Capital allowances for flats over shops (2001)
IR2008	ISAs, PEPs and TESSAs (2002)
IR2009	Why pay cash? (2001)
IR2010	Paying tax and NIC electronically (2004)
CGT1	Capital gains tax – An introduction (2003)
CGT1/FS1	Capital gains tax – A quick guide (2004)
IHT2	IHT on lifetime gifts (2004)

IHT3	IHT – An introduction (2004)
IHT4	Notes on informal calculations of IHT (2003). Obtainable from Inland Revenue, Ferrers House, PO Box 38, Castle Meadow Road, Nottingham NG2 1BB (0845 302 0900); Inland Revenue, Level 3, Dorchester House, 52–58 Great Victoria Street, Belfast BT2 7QL (0845 302 0900); Inland Revenue, Meldrum House, 15 Drumsheugh Gardens, Edinburgh EH3 7UG (0845 302 0900); or from the Stationery Orderline (0845 234 1000)
IHT8	Alterations to an inheritance following a death (2004). Obtainable as IHT4
IHT11	IHT – Payment of IHT from National Savings or British Government Stock (2004). Obtainable as IHT4)
IHT14	IHT – The personal representatives' responsibilities (2004) Obtainable as IHT4
IHT15	IHT – How to calculate the liability (1996). Internet only
IHT16	IHT – Settled property (2004). Obtainable as IHT4
IHT17	IHT – Businesses, farms and woodlands (2004). Obtainable as IHT4
IHT18	IHT – Foreign aspects (2004). Obtainable as IHT4
IHT19	IHT – Delivery of a reduced Inland Revenue account (2003)
SO1	Stamp duty on buying a freehold house in England, Wales or NI (2000)
SO1 (Scot)	Stamp duty on buying land or buildings in Scotland (2002)
SO2	Stamp Office customers promise and service information (2000)
SO3	If things go wrong – Complaints and lost documents (2000)
SO5	Common stamp duty forms and how to complete them (2002)
SO5 (Scot)	Common Scottish stamp duty forms and how to complete them (1996)
SO6	A short history of stamp duties (1996)
SO7	Stamp duty and leases (2000)
SO7 (Scot)	Stamp duty and leases in Scotland (2002)
SO8	Stamp duty on agreements and securing short tenancies (2002)
SO10	Stamp duty interest and penalties (2001)
SO11	Stamp duty and charities (1997)

SO99	Change to stamp duty from 1 October 1999 (2000)
SD1	SDLT: Enquiries into land transaction returns (2003)
SD2	SDLT: A quick guide to buying property (2003)
SD3	SDLT: A guide to leases (2003)
SD4	SDLT: A brief guide for practitioners (2003)
SD5	SDLT in Scotland: A brief guide for practitioners (2003)
SD7	SDLT: Penalties for late land transaction returns (2004)
480	Expenses and benefits – A tax guide (2004)
490	Employee travel – A tax and NICs guide for employers (2003)
AO1	How to complain about the Inland Revenue (2003)
CH24A	Child benefit and guardian's allowance – If you think our decision is wrong (2003)
CSS1	Customer service standards (2002)
CTSA/BK3	A modern system for corporation tax payments (2003)
CTSA/BK4	A general guide to corporation tax self-assessment (2003)
CWG2	Employer's further guide to PAYE and NIC (2004)
CWL2	NICs for self-employed people. Class 2 and Class 4 (2003)
CWL4	Fund-raising events: exemption for charities and other qualifying bodies (2001)
CWL5	The voluntary arrangements service (2002)
E10	Finishing the tax year up to 5 April 2004 (2004)
E11	Starting the tax year from 5 April 2004 (2004)
E12	PAYE and NICs rates and limits for 2004/5 (2004)
E13	Day-to-day payroll (2004)
E14	What to do if your employee is sick (2004)
E15	Pay and time off work for parents (2004)
E16	Pay and time off work for adoptive parents (2004)
E24	Tips, gratuities, service charges and troncs (2004)
FS1	Factsheet: Allowance restrictions (2003)
FS1 (MCA)	Married couple's allowance restrictions (2002)
FEU50	A guide to paying foreign entertainers (2000)
P3	PAYE: Understanding your tax code (2003)
P3(IB)	Incapacity benefit – PAYE: Understanding your tax code (2003)
P/SE/1	Thinking of working for yourself? (2004)

PSO3	Occupational pension schemes – A guide for trustees of small self-administered schemes (2001). Obtainable as IR76
SA/BK4	Self-assessment – A general guide to keeping records (2003)
SA/BK6	Self-assessment – Penalties for late returns (2003)
SA/BK7	Self-assessment – Surcharges for late payment of tax (2003)
SA/BK8	Self-assessment – Your guide (2004)
SALF	Self-assessment. The legal framework (2003)
SV1	Shares valuation – An introduction (2004). Obtainable as IHT4
WTC1	Child tax credit and working tax credit: An introduction (2002)
WTC2	Child tax credit and working tax credit: A guide (2003)
WTC3	Tax credit penalties: How tax credit examinations are settled (2004)
WTC4	Tax credit penalties: How tax credit enquiries are settled (2004)
WTC5	Child tax credit and working tax credit: Help with the costs of childcare (2004)
WTC/E6	Working tax credit paid with wages (2003)
WTC6	Child tax credit and working tax credit: Other types of help (2003)
WTC AP	Child tax credit and working tax credit: How to appeal against a tax credit decision or award (2003)

Business Economic Notes

1	Travel Agents (1990)
2	Road Haulage (1995)
3	The Lodging Industry (1990)
4	Hairdressers (1990)
5	Waste Materials Reclamation and Disposal (1990)
6	Funeral Directors (1990)
7	Dentists (1990)
8	Florists (1990)
9	Licensed Victuallers (1988)
10	The Jewellery Trade (1990)
11	Electrical Retailers (1990)
12	Antiques and Fine Art Dealers (1990)

13	Fish and Chip Shops (1990)
14	The Pet Industry (1990)
15	Veterinary Surgeons (1990)
16	Catering – General (1990)
17	Catering – Restaurants (1990)
18	Catering – Fast Foods, Cafes and Snack-Bars (1990)
19	Farming – Stock Valuation for IT Purposes (1993)
20	Insurance Brokers and Agents (1994)
21	Residential Rest and Nursing Homes (1994)
22	Dispensing Chemists (1995)
23	Driving Instructors (1997)
24	Independent Fishmongers (1997)
25	Taxicabs and Private Hire Vehicles (1997)
26	Confectioners, Tobacconists and Newsagents (1997)

Obtainable as IR 67. Price £1.60 each for Issues 1–22, £2 each for Issues 23 onwards

Revenue tax bulletin

Published bi-monthly for an annual subscription. Freely available on the internet.

National Insurance contributions leaflets

The leaflets listed below are issued by the Inland Revenue and are available free of charge. Most are available on the Inland Revenue internet site at www.inlandrevenue.gov.uk or can be obtained from your local Inland Revenue office.

CA01	NIC for employees (2004)
CA02	NIC for self-employed people with small earnings (2004)
CA04	Class 2 and Class 3 NIC – Direct Debit (2004)
CA07	Unpaid and late paid contributions (2004)
CA08	NIC voluntary contributions (2004)
CA09	NIC for widows and widowers (2003)

CA10	NIC for divorcees (2003)
CA11	NIC for share fishermen (2003)
CA12	NIC – Training for further employment and your NI records (2003)
CA13	NIC for women with reduced elections (2004)
CA14	Termination of Contracted-out Pension Employment (Salary Related Schemes) (2002)
CA14A	Termination of Contracted-out Pension Employment (Money Purchases Schemes) (2002)
CA14C	Contracted-out guidance for salary related pension schemes and salary related overseas schemes
CA14D	Contracted-out guidance for money purchase pension schemes and money purchase overseas schemes
CA14E	Contracted-out guidance for mixed benefit pension schemes and mixed benefit overseas schemes
CA14F	Technical guidance on Contracted-out decision making and appeals (2003)
CA15	Cessation of Contracted-out Pension Schemes (2003)
CA16	Appropriate Personal Pension Scheme Manual – Procedural Guidance (2003)
CA16A	Appropriate Personal Pension Scheme Manual – Guidance for Scheme Managers (2002)
CA17	Employee's guide to minimum contributions (2002). Available from Inland Revenue NIC Office, Services to Pensions Industry, Benton Park View, Newcastle upon Tyne NE98 1ZZ (0845 915 0150)
CA19	Using the Accrued GMP Liability Service (2003)
CA20	Using the Contracted-out Contributions/Earnings Information Service (2003)
CA21	Using the NI Number/Date of Birth Checking Service (2004)
CA22	Contracted-out data transactions using magnetic media (2002)
CA23	NIC for mariners (2001)
CA24	NIC for masters and employers of mariners (2001)
CA25	Agencies and people working through agencies (2003)
CA26	NIC for examiners, moderators and invigilators, lecturers, teachers and instructors (2003)

CA30	Statutory Sick Pay – Manual for employers (2003)
CA33	Employer's Manual on Class 1A NICs on cars and fuel (2004)
CA37	Simplified deductions scheme for employers (2004)
CA42	Foreign-going mariners' deep-sea fisherman's contributions for employers (2004)
CA44	NI for company directors (2004)
CA50	Making year end returns on tape or disc (1999)
CA51/52	Submitting year end returns on magnetic media – Technical guide (2004)
CA65	NIC for people working for embassies, consulates and overseas employers (2003)
CA72	NIC-deferring payment (2004)
CA75	Resolving benefit involved cases (2001)
CA76	NI abroad – A guide for employers of employees from abroad (2001)
CA82	If you think our decision is wrong (2001)
CA84	Stakeholder Pension Scheme Manual (2002)
CA85	Contracted-out stakeholder pension scheme manual (2003)
CA86	Employee's guide to Statutory Sick Pay (2004)
CA87	NIC and the Welsh Language (2000)
CA88	Payroll cleansing – What it is and what it can do for you (2002)
CA89	Payroll cleansing – A free service offered by the Inland Revenue (2003)
CA92	Services to pensions industry – An information guide (2004)
CA1437	Employer's guide to centralised payments of NIC (2001)
CWG2	Employer's further guide to PAYE and NICs (2004)
CWG5	Class 1A NICs benefits in kind – A guide for employers (2004)
P/SE/1	Starting your own business? (2004)
CWL2	NIC for self-employed people – Class 2 and 4 (2003)
NI38	Social security abroad – NICs, social security benefits, healthcare in certain overseas countries (2001)
NI132	NI for employers of people working abroad (2002)
OC SS1	NIC office: Our customer service standards (2003)
RD171	Shortfall in NICs – To pay or not to pay (2004)

92 Tax planning do's

- Buy your own house as soon as you can. Historically, houses have been a good investment. Any capital gain will be tax free. However, by the same token there are no tax allowances for any losses on sale.
- Make sure you have got good pension and life assurance cover and keep the situation constantly under review.
- Make use (if you can afford to) of the £3,000 tax-free annual capital transfer (i.e. give this sum away Inheritance-Tax-free each year) and if you did not use up last year's allowance, you can give away an additional £3,000.
- Always claim your personal and other tax allowances. This should normally be dealt with for you by the Inland Revenue, but you should keep the matter under annual review (e.g. have you passed retirement age? This is relevant because all sorts of considerations need to be taken into account, such as increased personal allowances and the fact that you will be receiving a state pension).
- Claim all business expenses you are entitled to against any business profits – always keep a chit for petty cash expenses. If you don't, how will your accountant know you have incurred that particular expense?
- Pay your spouse properly for any work he does in your business. In the 2005/06 tax year, remember that he can earn £4,895 tax free, although payments over this sum will involve him paying National Insurance contributions.
- Consult with your stockbroker in order to make sure you take advantage of the annual £8,500 Capital Gains Tax relief, i.e. if you can make a gain of this size, it will be tax free.
- Make a Will. Consult Lawpack' s *Wills, Power of Attorney & Probate Guide* or take legal advice.
- Think carefully about providing funds to pay any Inheritance Tax on death (term assurance isn't very expensive).
- Plan ahead and, wherever possible, let your accountant know of your plans/wishes so that you can be advised on any tax implications.

- Divide your assets and income with your spouse so that the best use is made of the independent taxation rules.
- Let an independent financial adviser give you the equivalent of a financial 'medical examination'.
- Ask your accountant to give a rough idea of your tax liability in January and July each year. Then divide the sum by 12 and start saving up for it by transferring the monthly figure to a deposit account. This way paying tax is much less painful.

93 Tax planning don'ts

- Don't enter into tax saving schemes, on the advice of either an accountant or anyone else, that run a long time. The law can change, your circumstances can change and either could make a nonsense of a long-term plan.
- Don't automatically trust trusts – refer to Lawpack's *Tax Answers at a Glance* book if you want more information on this matter. Be very careful about putting your money into trusts – don't set them up unless they will do exactly what you want. Trusts, which are set up to protect assets from the ravages of tax, can result not only in tax having to be paid, but also in assets having to be sold to pay the tax. The net result can be ghastly. Some trusts are very useful but tread very carefully – take professional advice.
- Don't give all your money away in order to save Inheritance Tax. If you do, what will you live on?
- Don't make your affairs too complicated. Keep your affairs simple and flexible so that you can (a) understand what is going on and (b) make any changes as and when you want.
- Don't try to cheat the taxman. Be honest in all your dealings. Keep proper records of all your transactions, especially cash receipts, and declare everything properly. If you don't, you will be found out.

CHAPTER 20

A summary

94 Employees, employers and company directors

- **Shares:** companies can offer shares to staff through a share option or share incentive scheme. The rules are complicated, but the chances of acquiring wealth in a tax-efficient way are very real. Talk to an accountant first.
- **Company car:** this still is the most popular fringe benefit, but the taxable benefit of having a car has increased so much in recent years that it is often better to give back the car and have the extra salary instead. If you are prepared to drive a smaller highly fuel-efficient car, it may still be beneficial to have a company car.
- **Company fuel:** this is now so heavily taxed that it will rarely be beneficial for a company to provide fuel to its employees. You should ensure that there is an agreement in writing which requires you to reimburse your company for any private fuel used. Better still, buy your own fuel and reclaim from the company that which is used for business. The best deal of all is to drive a van (see page 44).
- **Cheap loans to employees:** in many cases, no taxable benefit arises in the case of a loan of up to £5,000.
- **Meals:** in general, all benefits are taxable, but meals provided free of charge (or at low cost) in a canteen on the firm's premises are not taxable if they are available to staff generally.
- **Parties:** the Inland Revenue's practice is not to tax expenditure of up to £150 per head on the annual Christmas party or a similar function.
- **Accommodation:** a company may purchase a house for an employee to live in rent free. There may be a small amount of tax due on the value of the accommodation, etc., but the charge will be small in proportion to the benefits provided.
- **Payments to private healthcare schemes:** these are not taxable for lower-paid employees (defined as those receiving under £8,500 per annum, including the payments).
- **Employee rewards:** tax is not payable on financial rewards to staff for suggestions they may make on the running of a business. However, such 'suggestion schemes' must meet certain requirements.

- **Incentive awards:** employees can be given non-cash awards for meeting certain targets and, in addition, any tax that these might attract can be paid by the employer on the employees' behalf.
- **Occupational pension schemes:** while these speak for themselves and their benefits are well understood, it is sometimes overlooked that employees may increase their pension entitlements by making additional voluntary contributions (AVCs) to the scheme. AVCs attract tax relief at the highest rate of tax. Employers can also consider making pension schemes non-contributory. This way they can reduce payments they make to staff by the amount of the pension contributions the staff members have been making (in other words, the member of staff would be no worse off as a result of this), but the company would have less National Insurance contributions to pay on the lower salary figure.
- **Company directors' National Insurance contributions:** directors will be able to save themselves a little tax in the form of National Insurance contributions for themselves, if instead of receiving their pay in the form of salary they were to receive the equivalent sum in the form of rent for the company's use of property owned by the director, dividends on shares or interest from the loan made by the director to the company. However, you should seek professional advice.
- **Loans to directors:** it is illegal under company law for a company to lend any director money and, even if it is done, there are heavy tax penalties attached to this. Do consider the following points:
    1. Immediately before incorporation the business can take out a bank loan enabling you to withdraw a substantial sum in advance.
    2. You can arrange the capital structure of the company so that at least part of your investment is by way of a loan account against which you may be free to draw.
    3. It may be possible to keep certain assets (e.g. property used by the business) outside the company.
- **Other benefits:** provide tax-free benefits to your employees such as childcare, sports or recreation facilities.

95 Those moving house or changing jobs

If you move home in order to take up new employment, or even a new post within your existing organisation, the following costs can be reimbursed by your employer without any Income Tax charge arising, up to an overall maximum of £8,000:

1. Bridging finance
2. Legal and professional fees, stamp duty, removal costs and insurance
3. Travel and hotel costs
4. A reasonable subsistence allowance
5. A disturbance allowance

96 Those who are about to retire or who have retired

Golden handshakes – advance tax planning:

- You might ask your employer to pay part of any payment over £30,000 into your pension (within the limits of the scheme). The Revenue accepts that no tax charge arises on such payments and this could enhance the tax-free lump sum you receive from the scheme.
- If you are retiring and your total income will be significantly lower after retirement, it may be better to retire shortly after 5 April so that the taxable part of your golden handshake may be charged at a lower tax rate.

For the over 65s:

- Do remember that age allowance (a higher personal allowance) is available for those aged 65, and for those over 75 there is a higher-age allowance available.

97 The self-employed

The self-employed have considerably more flexibility in their tax saving arrangements than employers and employees, and those who are self-employed are probably well aware of the sort of advantages they may legitimately take. However, here are a few that should not be overlooked:

- If you are starting in business and need to draw all your profit to fund your living expenses, it may not be advisable to form a limited company straight away, even though there are considerable tax savings to be made, especially at lower levels of profit. As a self-employed trader, you have more flexibility and lower administrative costs. You can always incorporate later.
- A personal pension scheme is a most efficient way of diverting surplus profits into a tax-free lump sum and pension for the future.

Claimable expenses for the self-employed

Basic costs and general running expenses

Normally allowed – The cost of goods bought for resale and raw materials used in business. Advertising, delivery charges, heating, lighting, cleaning, rates, telephone. The rent of business premises. The replacement of small tools and special clothing. Postage, stationery, relevant books and magazines. Accountants' fees. Bank charges on business accounts. Fees to professional bodies. Security expenditure.

Not allowed – The initial cost of machinery, vehicles, equipment, permanent advertising signs – but you can claim capital allowances. The cost of buildings. Providing for anticipated expenses in the future.

Use of home for work

Normally allowed – The proportion of telephone, lighting, heating, cleaning, insurance. The proportion of rent and Council Tax, if you use part of your home exclusively for business – claiming ground rent and Council Tax may mean some Capital Gains Tax to pay if you sell your home – but this is unlikely.

Wages and salaries

Normally allowed – Wages, salaries, redundancy and leaving payments paid to employees. Pensions for past employees and their dependants. Staff training.

Not allowed – Your own wages or salary or that of any business partner. Your own drawings.

Tax and National Insurance

Normally allowed – Employer's National Insurance contributions for employees. Reasonable pay for your spouse, provided he is actually employed.

Not allowed – Income Tax. Capital Gains Tax. Inheritance Tax. Your own National Insurance contributions.

Entertaining

Normally allowed – Entertainment of own staff (e.g. a Christmas party).

Not allowed – Any other business entertaining.

Pre-trading

Normally allowed – Revenue business expenditure incurred within five years before starting to trade.

Gifts

Normally allowed – Gifts costing up to £50 a year to each person so long as the gift advertises your business (or things it sells). Gifts (whatever their value) to employees.

Not allowed – Food, drink, tobacco or vouchers for goods given to anyone other than employees.

Travelling

Normally allowed – Hotel and travelling expenses on business trips. Travel between different places of work. The running costs of your own car – whole of cost if used wholly for business, proportion if used privately too.

Not allowed – Travel between home and business. The cost of buying a car or van (but you can claim capital allowances).

If a business leases a car costing more than £12,000, part of the leasing cost is disallowed for tax purposes. The rules are complicated, but, in principle, the more expensive the car you lease, the smaller the sum that you will be allowed to claim as a tax deduction in your accounts.

Interest payments

Normally allowed – The interest on overdrafts and loans for business purposes.

Not allowed – The interest on capital paid or credited to partners.

Hire purchase

Normally allowed – Hire charge part of instalments (i.e. the amount you pay less the cash price).

Not allowed – Cash price of what you are buying on hire purchase (but you may get capital allowances).

Hiring

Normally allowed – Reasonable charge for hire of capital goods, including cars.

Insurance

Normally allowed – Business insurance (e.g. employer's liability, fire and theft, motor, insuring employees' lives).

Not allowed – Your own life insurance.

Trade marks

Normally allowed – Fees paid to register a trademark, design or patent.

Not allowed – The cost of buying a patent from someone else (but you may get capital allowances).

Legal costs

Normally allowed – The costs of recovering debts, defending business rights, preparing service agreements, appealing against rates, renewing a lease for a period not exceeding 50 years (but not if a premium is paid).

Not allowed – Expenses (including stamp duty) for acquiring land, buildings or leases. Fines and other penalties for breaking the law.

Repairs

Normally allowed – Normal repairs and maintenance to premises or equipment.

Not allowed – The cost of additions, alterations, improvements (but you may get capital allowances).

Debts

Normally allowed – Specific provisions for debts and debts written off.

Not allowed – General reserve for bad or doubtful debts.

Subscriptions

Normally allowed – Payments which secure benefits for your business or staff. Payments to societies that have arrangements with the Inland Revenue (in some cases only a proportion). However, do watch for possible National Insurance contributions.

Not allowed – Payments to political parties, churches, charities contributions (but small gifts to local churches and charities may be allowed).

98 Personal taxpayers, both rich and poor

High-rate taxpayers

For those with high income (i.e. into the 40 per cent tax band), and particularly if surplus to requirements, funds can be diverted to the following havens for tax advantages either on initial payment or at a later date:

- **Life assurance:** investing in a 'with profits' endowment policy that will run for at least ten years can produce a good tax-free return.
- **National Savings Certificates:** these can produce a good tax-free income. It is always a good idea to keep aware of what National Savings Schemes have on offer.
- **Perks in quoted shares:** many quoted shares now offer perks to their shareholders and these are entirely tax free.

- **National Insurance:** there is a maximum total of National Insurance contributions you need to pay. If you have more than one source of employment earnings and you are in danger of paying more than the maximum, why not defer Class 1 contributions on one of the employments to avoid making an overpayment?
- **Investments** in:

  1. pensions;
  2. the Enterprise Investment Scheme (EIS);

     You can invest up to £200,000 in Enterprise Investment Scheme (EIS) shares and you will get Income Tax relief of 20 per cent on that amount. When you sell, you get full Capital Gains Tax relief (presently 40 per cent). There is a minimum investment of £500. The EIS replaced the Business Expansion Scheme, which used to give Income Tax relief of 40 per cent.

     Half of an investment made before 6 October may be carried back to the previous tax year for Income Tax purposes (up to a maximum of £25,000).

     You must hold your Enterprise Investment Scheme shares for at least three years or the relief will be withdrawn (five years in the case of shares issued before 6 April 2000).

     Any loss you make on the sale of the shares is available against either capital gains or income.

     You must not be connected with the company (i.e. hold over 30 per cent of the shares or be an employee), although you can become a director of the company and still qualify for EIS relief as long as you were not connected with the company before the shares were issued.

     Rollover relief: in addition to the above, if you have made a capital gain this year, and if you reinvest all that gain in the purchase of EIS shares, you can thereby defer all the Capital Gains Tax payable this year on that gain until you sell your EIS shares.
  3. a Venture Capital Trust (see page 13);
  4. unquoted shares.

For low earners

Young earners

Young people starting in employment have little scope for tax saving (usually because they have a low income), but they should not overlook the favourable Capital Gains Tax treatment available for those who purchase their main residence. Very few people have ever regretted purchasing their own residence.

Other low earners

Do not forget if you are a low earner, whether in employment or self-employment, you may be able to avoid either Class 1 or Class 2 National Insurance contributions. You should not claim exemption from Class 2 contributions on the basis of low earnings unless you are already paying contributions on another source of income. If you don't pay, you build up no entitlement to benefits or pension rights. £2.10 per week is a small sum to pay to safeguard this entitlement.

99 Children

Surplus after-tax income transferred by parents to their children is usually non-taxable in the hands of the child. However, where children earn income exceeding £100 in any tax year on capital provided by their parents, the whole income will be counted as that of their parents.

As we've said before, make sure that savings accounts with building societies or banks in children's names are paying interest gross. Ask the bank for, and complete, Form R85, which certifies the children as non-taxpayers.

100 Capital Gains Tax planning

- **Married couples:** each spouse will be taxed on his own gains and receives a non-transferable annual exemption of £8,500.

- **Annual exemptions:** do remember to maximise them. To this end you could delay disposals until after the next 5 April if you have already used your current exemption or, alternatively, bring forward planned disposals to before 6 April if you have not yet used your exemption, or split the disposals of an asset, such as blocks of shares, to straddle 5 April in order to obtain the benefit of two years' exemptions. Consider whether you can wait until after 5 April to make the sales so as to delay the tax payment by a further 12 months.
- **Assets of negligible value:** if you hold an asset (e.g. shares in a company) which has lost most of its value, you may be able to claim the capital loss now against any Capital Gains Tax. Ask your tax inspector if he will allow the loss.
- **Loans and guarantees:** you may obtain relief for losses on loans and guarantees made to people who have used the money wholly for the purpose of their business. Relief is not available if the loss or guarantee arises through your own act or omission or where the borrower is your husband or wife.
- **Gifts:** all gifts are exempt from stamp duty.
- **Gifts between spouses:** no capital gain or loss arises on gifts between husband and wife, but the recipient takes over the other spouse's acquisition date and original value.
- **Gifts to charities:** because these are exempt from Capital Gains Tax it is often better, if you intend making a charitable donation of an asset which would realise a gain on disposal (e.g. shares), to consider donating the asset rather than the equivalent amount of cash. The charity may subsequently sell the shares and realise the gain free of tax because of its privileged status.
- **Holdover relief for gifts:** this is restricted to business assets, heritage property and property on which there is an immediate charge to Inheritance Tax. Do not always claim holdover relief – it is sometimes cheaper to pay a small amount of tax than to hold over the tax bill of some considerably greater sum to the future.
- **Assets to children:** if you have assets which you expect will increase in value over a period of time, consider giving them to your children now.

- **Main residence:** no Capital Gains Tax is payable on the disposal of your home. Taking in a lodger does not affect your main residence relief but letting the property does.

101 Inheritance Tax planning

- It is now possible to give away £275,000 every seven years without a charge to Inheritance Tax arising. However, there may be Capital Gains Tax on the gift, so take professional advice.
- There is, of course, tapering relief on gifts so that, as the years up to seven slip by, the tax bill does reduce significantly.
- It is important to remember, in planning to reduce the Inheritance Tax bill upon your death, not to give away too much unless you can genuinely afford to do so. If you wish to make a gift of your family home but also wish to continue living in it, you must either pay full market rent for the privilege or consult a specialist Inheritance Tax adviser who can provide a sophisticated planning scheme to circumvent the 'reservation of benefit' rules. With no Capital Gains Tax arising on death it is sometimes better to let properties pass on death rather than before. However, this matter must be carefully weighed up before a decision is made.
- Lifetime gifts: gifts between husband and wife are exempt from Inheritance Tax planning.
- Remember, you can give away the annual Inheritance-Tax-free exempt sum of £3,000, which may be doubled up if exemption was not used in the previous year.
- Gifts of up to £250 per year to an individual are tax free.
- Gifts out of surplus income are tax free; take professional advice on this.
- Wedding gifts up to certain limits are tax free.
- Term assurance is a sensible means of protecting a gift that has been made should tax become due as a result of death within seven years.
- Always make a Will and build the necessary tax planning points into it. Discuss this with your solicitor.

- Special reliefs: generally, business assets attract some measure of relief, as does woodland and agricultural property. Agricultural property without a right to vacant possession attracts a smaller relief.
- Trusts for younger children: this is a complicated subject and advice must be sought from your solicitor.
- Doubling up the main residence relief: it does not make good sense for you to buy a house or flat for your adult children to live in since any gain you make on its subsequent sale will be chargeable to Capital Gains Tax. Instead, consider providing your child with the necessary funds to make the purchase in his own name and you could do this by making an interest-free loan which you reduce each year by the annual £3,000 exemption.
- Incorporation of a growing business: it may be advantageous to give shares in the company to your children and/or grandchildren soon after incorporation when their value is relatively low.

Appendix

Tax rates and allowances for 2005/06

Income Tax			Taxable Income		
		Band	From	To	Rate
		2,020	0	2,090	10%
		30,310	2,091	32,400	22%
		over	32,400		40%
Capital Gains Tax (for individuals)			First	8,500	Exempt
			Balance taxed at 20% and/or 40%		
	Taper relief for long-term gains. This is now complicated – consult an accountant for details.				
Corporation Tax		Band	From	To	Rate
		10,000	0	10,000	0%
		40,000	10,001	50,000	23.75%
		250,000	50,001	300,000	19%
		1,200,000	300,001	1,500,000	32.75%
		over	1,500,001		30%
Inheritance Tax (on death)		Band	From	To	Rate
		275,000	0	275,000	0%
		over	275,000		40%
Personal Allowances	Personal				4,895
	Personal (aged 65 to 74)				7,090
	Married Couples (65 to 74)*#				5,905
	Personal over 75				7,220
	Married Couples over 75*#				5,975
	All 4 higher age allowances are only available for incomes up to £19,500 in 2005/06				
	* = relief restricted to 10% # = husband or wife must be born before 6 April 1937				
National Insurance					
Class 1 (Employment)	Employee (not contracted out)				
	Earnings per week				
	Up to £94				Nil
	£94 to £630				11%
	Over £630				1%
	Employer (not contracted out)				
	Up to £94				Nil
	Over £94				12.8%
Class 2 (Self-Employment)	(The old weekly stamp)				£2.10
	No contributions due if profits below £4,345				
Class 4 (Self-Employment)	8% on profits between		£4,895	and	£32,760
	1% on profits over £32,760				
State Pension				Week	Year
		Single		82.05	£4,266.60
		Married		131.20	£6,822.40
		Over 80		0.25	£13.00
VAT	Threshold with effect from 1 April 2005				£60,000
	Rate				17.5%
Quarterly Scale Charge for Motoring				Engine Size	
		Fuel	To 1400cc	1401–2000	Over 2000
		Petrol	36.64	46.32	68.08
		Diesel	35.15	35.15	44.68
Taxable Car Benefits	The taxable Fuel Benefit is the same percentage as the Car Benefit, and applied to £14,400.				
	Car Benefit is now based on CO_2 emissions. Visit www.inlandrevenue.gov.uk to find out how to calculate Car and Fuel Benefits.				
				Age at End of Tax Year	
			Less than 4 years old		Over 4 years old
		Vans	£500		£350
Car Mileage Allowance	All Engine Sizes				
Up to 10,000 miles pa	40p				
Over 10,000 miles pa	25p				

Tax rates and allowances for 2004/05

Income Tax		Taxable Income		
	Band	From	To	Rate
	2,020	0	2,020	10%
	29,380	2,021	31,400	22%
	over	31,400		40%
Capital Gains Tax (for individuals)		First	8,200	Exempt
		Balance taxed at 20% and/or 40%		
	Taper relief for long-term gains. This is now complicated – consult an accountant for details.			
Corporation Tax	Band	From	To	Rate
	10,000	0	10,000	0%
	40,000	10,001	50,000	23.75%
	250,000	50,001	300,000	19%
	1,200,000	300,001	1,500,000	32.75%
	over	1,500,001		30%
Inheritance Tax (on death)	Band	From	To	Rate
	263,000	0	263,000	0%
	over	263,000		40%
Personal Allowances	Personal			4,745
	Personal (aged 65 to 74)			6,830
	Married Couples (66 to 74)*#			5,725
	Personal over 75			6,950
	Married Couples over 75*#			5,795
	All 4 higher age allowances are only available for incomes up to £18,900 in 2004/05			
	* = relief restricted to 10% # = husband or wife must be born before 6 April 1937			
National Insurance				
Class 1 (Employment)	Employee (not contracted out)			
	Earnings per week			
	Up to £91			Nil
	£91 to £610			11%
	Over £610			1%
	Employer (not contracted out)			
	Up to £91			Nil
	Over £91			12.8%
Class 2 (Self-Employment)	(The old weekly stamp)			£2.05
	No contributions due if profits below £4,215			
Class 4 (Self-Employment)	8% on profits between	£4,745	and	£31,720
	1% on profits over £31,720			
State Pension			Week	Year
	Single		79.60	£4,139.20
	Married		127.25	£6,617.00
	Over 80		0.25	£13.00
VAT	Threshold			£58,000
	Rate			17.5%
Quarterly Scale Charge for Motoring			Engine Size	
	Fuel	To 1400cc	1401–2000	Over 2000
	Petrol	34.55	43.63	64.34
	Diesel	32.17	32.17	40.65
Taxable Car Benefits	The Fuel Benefit is now based on CO_2 emissions.			
	The Car Benefit is now based on CO_2 emissions. Visit www.inlandrevenue.gov.uk to find out how to calculate Car and Fuel Benefits.			
		Age at End of Tax Year		
		Less than 4 years old		Over 4 years old
	Vans	£500		£350
Car Mileage Allowance	All Engine Sizes			
Up to 10,000 miles pa	40p			
Over 10,000 miles pa	25p			

Index

D

E

M

N

O

S

MORE BOOKS AVAILABLE FROM **LAWPACK**

Residential Lettings

Are you thinking of letting a flat or a house? This guide steers anyone who intends – or already is – letting property through the legal and practical issues involved. It provides all the up-to-date information and tips that a would-be landlord needs. It will also alert existing landlords to the points of good practice that make a letting successful, and the legal obligations that they may not be aware of.

Code B622 | ISBN 1 904053 90 4 | Paperback | 153 x 234mm | 160pp | £11.99 | 5th edition

The Buy-to-Let Bible

Low mortgage rates and under-performance by traditional savings and investment products means that property has never looked a better way to invest for the future. Author Ajay Ahuja divulges the practical and financial techniques that have made him a millionaire. It covers finding the right property, the right mortgage lender, the right tenant, legal issues and tax.

Code B637 | ISBN 1 904053 91 2 | Paperback | 153 x 234mm | 256pp | £11.99 | 3rd edition

The Seven Pillars of Buy-to-Let Wisdom

In his first, bestselling buy-to-let book, *The Buy-to-Let Bible* author and buy-to-let millionaire Ajay Ahuja provided the basics of successful buy-to-let. Ajay has now written 'further reading' for the buy-to-let investor, *The Seven Pillars of Buy-to-let Wisdom*, that explains in depth how to get the most from your investment by examining the seven fundamentals of successful buy-to-let property management.

Code B447 | ISBN 1 904053 42 4 | Paperback | 153 x 234mm | 144pp | £9.99 | 1st edition

To order, visit **www.lawpack.co.uk** or call **020 7394 4040**

MORE BOOKS AVAILABLE FROM **LAWPACK**

Book-Keeping Made Easy

This guide provides the new business owner with an understanding of the fundamental principles of book-keeping, showing how to set up accounts and how to benefit from the information they contain. Includes procedures for the sole proprietor and small business, accounting for growing businesses, double-entry book-keeping, ledgers, payroll and final accounts.

Code B516 | ISBN 1 904053 85 8 | Paperback | 153 x 234mm | 104pp | £10.99 | 2nd edition

Business Agreements Made Easy

This book's primary focus is business-to-business contracts for supply of services and/or goods with limited reference to business-to-consumer contracts. It explains the key commercial and legal issues which occur throughout a 'contract lifecycle' (i.e. from pre-contract stage to negotiation of contract to end of contract) with suggested actions and steps.

Code B519 | ISBN 1 904053 84 X | Paperback | 153 x 234mm | 144pp | £11.99 | 1st edition

Business Letters Made Easy

Business Letters Made Easy provides an invaluable source of 199 ready-drafted letters for a range of business situations. Each letter has a useful commentary, explaining when to use a particular letter and helping you choose the right turn of phrase. This book takes the headache and time-wasting out of letter writing, and provides you with letters that get results!

Code B520 | ISBN 1 904053 87 4 | Paperback | 153 x 234mm | 288pp | £12.99 | 1st edition

To order, visit **www.lawpack.co.uk** or call **020 7394 4040**

MORE BOOKS AVAILABLE FROM **LAWPACK**

Running Your Own Business Made Easy

You have a business idea that you want to put into action, but you also want advice on the realities of setting up and running a business: this Made Easy guide is for you. It takes you through the business-creation process, from assessing your aptitude and ideas, to funding and business plans.

Code B511 | ISBN 1 905261 05 5 | Paperback | 153 x 234mm | 128pp | £9.99 | 3rd edition

Proper Coffee

Management tomes abound but they can be turgid to wade through. This book provides a refreshing alternative for the small business. It provides succinct, practical advice on how to raise the bottom line and increase profitability, without working any harder.

Code B451 | ISBN 1 904053 86 6 | Paperback | 153 x 234mm | 150pp | £9.99 | 1st edition

Tax Answers at a Glance 2005/06

We all need to get to grips with the array of taxes now levied by the government. Compiled by award-winning tax experts and presented in question-and-answer format, this handbook provides a useful and digestible summary of Income Tax, Capital Gains Tax, Inheritance Tax, pensions, self-employment, partnerships, Corporation Tax, Stamp Duty/Land Tax, VAT, and more.

Code B625 | ISBN 1 904053 76 9 | Paperback | 153 x 234mm | 208pp | £9.99 | 5th edition

To order, visit **www.lawpack.co.uk** or call **020 7394 4040**

MORE BOOKS AVAILABLE FROM LAWPACK

301 Legal Forms, Letters & Agreements

Our best-selling form book is now in its eighth edition. It is packed with forms, letters and agreements for legal protection in many situations. It provides a complete do-it-yourself library of 301 ready-to-use legal documents, for business or personal use. Areas covered include loans and borrowing, buying and selling, employment, transfers and assignments and residential tenancy.

Code B402 | ISBN 1 904053 66 1 | Paperback | A4 | 384pp | £19.99 | 8th edition

Personnel Manager

A book of more than 200 do-it-yourself forms, contracts and letters to help your business manage its personnel records. Areas covered include recruitment and hiring, employment contracts and agreements, handling new employees, personnel management, performance evaluation and termination of employment.

Code B417 | ISBN 1 905261 04 7 | Paperback | A4 | 272pp | £14.99 | 4th edition

Ready-Made Company Minutes & Resolutions

Maintaining good, up-to-date records of company meetings and resolutions is not only good practice but also a legal requirement, whatever size your company is. This book of forms makes compiling minutes of board and shareholder meetings straightforward. It includes more than 125 commonly-required resolutions and minutes to save you time and effort.

Code B616 | ISBN 1 904053 73 4 | Paperback | A4 | 184pp | £14.99 | 3rd edition

To order, visit **www.lawpack.co.uk** or call **020 7394 4040**

Visit the new Lawpack website and order online at www.lawpack.co.uk

What's new?

We've tried to retain the ease of use of our old site, while offering much more in terms of free legal information, more comprehensive product descriptions to give a true idea of what you're buying and links to qualified solicitors and legal resources if our products aren't appropriate for your situation.

Comprehensive product listings

First and foremost, Lawpack is a DIY legal publisher, and our ever-expanding range of easy-to-use titles is brought to life on the new website with extensive product overviews, author biographies, full content details and recommendations of other complementary titles in our range.